The Golden Age of Video Games

· ·

The Birth of a Multi-Billion Dollar Industry

The Golden Age of Video Games

....

The Birth of a Multi-Billion Dollar Industry

Roberto Dillon

....

CRC Press
Taylor & Francis Group
Boca Raton London New York

CRC Press is an imprint of the
Taylor & Francis Group, an **informa** business

AN A K PETERS BOOK

A K Peters/CRC Press
Taylor & Francis Group
6000 Broken Sound Parkway NW, Suite 300
Boca Raton, FL 33487-2742

First issued in hardback 2017

ISBN-13: 978-1-4398-7323-6 (pbk)
ISBN-13: 978-1-138-42786-0 (hbk)

Library of Congress Cataloging-in-Publication Data

Dillon, Roberto.
  The golden age of video games : the birth of a multi-billon dollar industry / Roberto Dillon.
      p. cm.
  Summary: "This book focuses on the history of video games, consoles, and home computers from the very beginning until the mid-nineties, which started a new era in digital entertainment. The text features the most innovative games and introduces the pioneers who developed them. It offers brief analyses of the most relevant games from each time period. An epilogue covers the events and systems that followed this golden age while the appendices include a history of handheld games and an overview of the retro-gaming scene"—Provided by publisher.
  Includes bibliographical references and index.
  ISBN 978-1-4398-7323-6 (pbk.)
  1. Video games—History. 2. Electronic games—History. 3. Computer games—History. 4. Video games industry. I. Title.
  GV1469.3.D55 2011
  794.8--dc22   2011005062

Visit the Taylor & Francis Web site at
http://www.taylorandfrancis.com

and the CC Press Web site at
http://www.crcpress.com

To my parents, Giorgio and Elisa,

for having introduced me

to video games and computers

at an early age

(and for not having scolded me

too harshly when I was

playing instead of studying).

Contents

● ● ● ● ● ● ●

Part I

Part II

Part III

Epilogue

Foreword

· · · · · · ·

Nolan Bushnell had the idea of a video game. Just because a video game industry *didn't* exist didn't mean that it *shouldn't* exist. Nolan and I would have to create it.

Long before there was a video game industry, there were several brilliant engineers who designed games that were played on a cathode ray tube (CRT), which is a TV without a tuner. Early endeavors required computers that were much too expensive to be commercially viable. The video game industry would have to wait.

There is a lot of controversy over just who invented the first "video game." Some say it was Ralph Baer while others say it was Nolan Bushnell. The truth is, it was Thomas Goldsmith Jr. and Estle Ray Man in 1947. The real question should be "Who created the video game *industry*?" Nolan and I get the credit for that one. Although *Computer Space* wasn't very successful, it did give birth to this industry. It took the arrival of *Pong* to give the industry significant life.

It should be noted that *Computer Space* has become quite a phenomenon. There are people and organizations that find this piece of work to be historical. They find these 40-year-old games and restore them to perfection. Some remember the 1973 movie *Soylent Green* only because it had a *Computer Space* in one of the scenes.

Bally Corporation of Chicago had paid Atari $24,000 to create a video game for them. That game became *Pong*, which they subsequently rejected. My question to Al Alcorn and Nolan Bushnell was "Do we want to go into production ourselves or do we want to go home?" None of us wanted to go home, so the adventure began.

The chronicling of video games goes back over 60 years, so this book involves a lot of painstaking research. Sometimes it is very hard to separate truth from myth and legend, but Professor Dillon has worked many hours doing just that.

Xbox, PS3, and Wii enthusiasts, along with those interested in technology, can get a lot of insight from this book. Sometimes it's just fun to know how all this stuff came to be what it is today.

Ted Dabney
Atari Cofounder

Preface

· · · · · · ·

Modern computers and electronic games were born roughly at the same time, though independently, in the 1940s. Several decades have passed since the early days of computers. Many home and business-oriented systems have emerged and faded into oblivion as technology has advanced at an incredible rate.

In this time, many books have been published on the history of computers and electronic games; in the last 10 years alone, many people have taken an interest in video game history and the subject is now even being taught at the university level. Indeed, the idea for this book came when I was preparing the Game History classes at the DigiPen Institute of Technology in Singapore and I started looking deeper into the literature on the subject, expanding my existing library. However, I couldn't find any single text on which to base my course, or to wholeheartedly recommend to my students. Some books were designed as luscious coffee table items, with many beautiful pictures, but were not very practical for serious study. Other books focused only on a specific branch of the industry, such as consoles, arcades, or a particular company or genre.

What I wanted, on the other hand, was something reasonably comprehensive yet agile and well balanced. I wanted to outline the history of both home computers and dedicated game machines, and to feature the most influential and innovative games while also introducing some of the pioneers to whom all of us owe a great debt. Last but not least, I wanted a book that was easy and entertaining to read. In other words, I wanted a book that wouldn't just be for study but that would be read and enjoyed by a broad range of people, any time or anywhere—on the bus or train, on the way to school, or on a relaxing vacation.

The Golden Age of Video Games focuses on the history of video games, consoles, and home computers from the very beginning until the mid-nineties, when some very important changes took place. Those changes were the definitive affirmation of IBM PCs as the standard home computer; the bankruptcy of previous home computer leader, Commodore; and the debut and rise of Sony's Playstation console. All together, they marked an end to the gaming world as it was known previously and started a new era in digital entertainment.

The book is structured in three different parts:

◘ Part I covers the very early steps of video games in research labs and universities and moves into the beginning of the gaming and home computers industry until 1982.

◘ Part II is dedicated to the infamous 1983 video game crash, the affirmation of the home computer market, and the start of the video game renaissance thanks to the Nintendo Entertainment System.

◘ Part III covers 16-bit systems and the different generations that emerged up to the mid-nineties.

Each part ends with a section titled Games That Pushed Boundaries. This section briefly discusses and analyzes some of the most relevant games that contributed, in one way or another, to the advancement of video games and, ultimately, defined them as the most influential entertainment medium of the last decades.

In addition to the three main parts of the book, an Epilogue section outlines the events and systems that followed the demise of Commodore and classic machines, and the Appendices provide a brief history of handheld devices and an overview of the retro game collecting scene that is now growing in popularity.

It is my hope that this book will provide an enjoyable read—not only to students of game development, but also to all retro game enthusiasts. I hope this book will help us to understand how the game industry developed through its short but intense history, as well as to remember the good old days when games looked much simpler but were still a lot of fun.

Roberto Dillon
June 1, 2010

Acknowledgments

● ● ● ● ● ● ● ● ● ● ● ● ●

Every book on an historical subject has to be thoroughly researched by checking countless sources and materials, and this book is no exception. To write it, I went through literally hundreds of computer and video game websites, magazines, and books mostly from the United States, UK, and my native country, Italy, in a never-ending quest to know more about this subject and to find accurate data. I extend my deepest thanks to all the journalists, writers, and passionate people who worked throughout the years to document games, systems, and everything related to this entertainment medium we all love so much and who now keep working to preserve its memory and legacy. Relevant references are listed in the Bibliography.

Special thanks to Ted Dabney for his kindness and invaluable feedback in the early Atari days. Many thanks to Davide Pasca, Matt Casanova, and Randy Knapp and to the editorial staff at A K Peters, in particular to Ms. Kara Ebrahim, for their fundamental help.

Last but not least, big thanks also to my wife, Jing, for her support, patience, and understanding while I was writing this book.

Timeline

• • • • • •

The Early Age: 1947–1976

1947:

◘ Thomas Goldsmith Jr. and Estle Ray Man patent the *CRT Amusement Device*, the first electronic game played by using TV technology.

1952:

◘ Alexander Douglas discusses his computer game *OXO* for his Ph.D. thesis at Cambridge University.

1958:

◘ *Tennis for Two* by Willy Higinbotham is showcased at Brookhaven National Labs, NY.

1961:

◘ At MIT, Stephen Russell and friends start programming *Spacewar!*.

1971:

◘ Nutting Associates releases *Computer Space* by Nolan Bushnell and Ted Dabney, the first commercial video game.

1972:

◘ Magnavox releases the Odyssey by Ralph Baer, the first home console.

◘ Nolan Bushnell and Ted Dabney found Atari.

◘ Atari releases its first product: coin operated *Pong* by Al Alcorn, the first hit in the video game industry.

1973:

◘ In the United States, Williams and Midway enter the video game business. Taito does the same in Japan.

1974:

◘ Namco distributes Atari's coin-ops in Japan.

1975:

◘ Atari releases *Home Pong*. Many imitators follow.

◘ Taito's *Gunfight* is distributed in the United States by Midway and is the first arcade game to use a CPU (added by Nutting Associates in the US version).

1976:

◘ Coleco *Telstar* games released.

◘ First cartridge-based video game console, Fairchild Channel F, is released.

◘ Bushnell sells Atari to Warner Communications for $28 million. The VCS is in the works under the codename Stella.

The Golden Age: 1977–1993

1977:

◘ Nintendo releases its first home video game systems in Japan.

◘ The Atari VCS is released.

◘ The Apple II and the Commodore PET are unveiled at the West Coast Computer Fair. Tandy's RadioShack releases the TRS-80 personal computer.

1978:

◘ Magnavox releases the Odyssey², distributed by Philips in Europe as the Videopac G7000.

◘ Taito's new game *Space Invaders* provokes a 100-¥ coin shortage in Japan.

1979:

◘ Mattel releases the Intellivision console.

◘ A game called *Adventure* is released for the VCS and the action/adventure genre is born, together with the first "easter egg."

◘ Atari enters the home computer market with the 400 and 800 models to compete with Apple.

◘ Vectorbeam/Cinematronics releases *Tail Gunner*, the first 3D game, in the arcades.

1980:

◘ Activision is formed to produce Atari VCS games. It is the first third-party software house.

◘ Namco releases *Puck-Man* in Japan, aka *Pac-Man* in the rest of the world.

◘ UK-based Sinclair releases the ZX-80, an extremely basic machine that can nonetheless be regarded as the first low-cost home computer.

◘ Commodore releases the VIC-20, under the name VIC-1001, in Japan to test the market.

1981:

◘ In January, Commodore officially releases the VIC-20, the first low-cost home color computer and the first one to break one million units sold.

◘ Sinclair releases the ZX-81, refining its previous model.

◘ Video game addiction starts to become a problem in many countries and games are often seen as detrimental to the youth. In the Philippines, on November 19, President Marcos bans video games, giving people two weeks to "surrender" any video game to the army and police forces. Violators faced a fine of $600 or 6 months to 12 years in jail. The ban was lifted a few years later.

1982:

◘ Cynex releases the Game Mate 2, the world's first wireless control joysticks, compatible with the Atari 2600 and Commodore VIC-20.

◘ The Commodore 64 is released.

◘ Sinclair releases the ZX-Spectrum.

◘ Board game giant Parker Brothers enters the video game market by producing cartridges for different systems.

◘ Coleco introduces the ColecoVision.

◘ Atari releases the 5200 Super System while restyling and renaming the VCS to the 2600.

1983:

◘ Due to a number of factors, the industry crashes in North America. Many companies go bankrupt within a couple of years. "Two or three years from now, video games will be considered a piece of history," according to Richard Stearns, VP for Consumer Electronics at Parker Bros.

- Atari dumps 14 truckloads of game cartridges and other computer equipment in a landfill in Alamogordo, New Mexico. A few million cartridges of *ET: The Extraterrestrial* are included.

- Cinematronics releases *Dragon's Lair* in the arcades.

- In Japan, Sega and Nintendo release the SG-1000 and the Famicom, respectively.

1984:

- Amstrad CPC is released to compete against the C64 and ZX Spectrum.

- Atari discontinues the 5200 system and releases the 7800 instead. The company is split in two and Jack Tramiel buys the consumer division, renaming it Atari Corp. The 7800 is soon pulled out and home computers become the main focus of the restructured company.

- Mattel closes its electronics division. Intellivision rights are sold for $20 million to the newly formed INTV Corp.

1985:

- At the Summer Consumer Electronics Show, Nintendo introduces the Nintendo Entertainment System (NES). The NES is later officially released in North America at a $125 price.

- Nintendo releases *Super Mario Bros.* for the NES. It will sell more than 40 million units worldwide.

- Commodore Amiga 1000 and Atari ST computers are released.

- Sega releases the Master System in Japan (under the name Mark III). North American release will follow in 1986.

1986:

- Atari re-releases the 7800 ProSystem in the United States (release in Europe will follow one year later) along with a slim version of the 2600, named 2600 Jr.

- Nintendo releases *The Legend of Zelda* and *Metroid* in Japan, both destined to become two of the most beloved game series ever.

- The First Computer Game Developers Conference (dubbed "Symposium") is organized and takes place in the home of famed game designer Chris Crawford.

1987:

- In Japan, NEC releases the PC Engine video game system (to be released in North America in 1989).

- Commodore releases the Amiga 500, the most successful model in the Amiga line.

- Konami releases *Metal Gear* for the MSX system in Japan while Square releases *Final Fantasy* for the Famicom.

1988:

- Nintendo of America debuts the *Nintendo Power* magazine in the United States, and 3.6 million copies are given away.

- Sega releases the MegaDrive in Japan (renamed Genesis for the American market where it was released in 1989).

- Sony officially enters the video game industry by designing and producing audio chips for the upcoming Nintendo Super Famicom system.

1989:

- Nintendo introduces the Game Boy handheld game system, selling it in bundle with *Tetris*.

- Atari introduces the Lynx handheld video game system.

- NEC releases a CD-ROM add-on for the PC Engine in Japan, turning it into the first console to use CD-ROM data.

1990:

- Nintendo releases the Super Famicom (renamed SNES outside of Japan) and owns 90% of the total video game market share worldwide.

- Commodore introduces the 64 Games System. It is a Commodore 64 computer without the keyboard and with the cartridge slot on top.

- NEC introduces the TurboExpress hand-held video game system in the United States.

1991:

- Sega debuts the Game Gear portable video game system.

- Nintendo and Sony announce a cooperation to develop a compact disk player for the Super Famicom. The deal breaks apart right after the announcement as Nintendo decides to partner with Philips instead. Sony will go its own way, leading to the PlayStation a few years later.

- Atari releases a new version of the Lynx, slashing the price to $99.

- Nintendo introduces the SNES in North America, priced at $199.95.

- Philips Electronics releases the CD-I multimedia system, using compact disks for games and other interactive applications. Price is $1,000.

- Hosted by AOL and developed by Beyond Software, *Neverwinter Nights* is the first Massively Multiplayer Online Role Playing Game (MMORPG) to break away from a text-only interface.

1992:

- Sega releases its CD add-on for the Genesis.

1993:

- Atari releases the Jaguar, its last system.

- Nintendo releases *Star Fox* for the SNES in the United States. The game is the first with the FX Chip for improved visuals and sounds.

- ID Software releases *Doom*, and PC gaming reaches new heights.

- Sega introduces a rating system for its video games: GA (general audience), MA-13 (mature, minimum age 13), and MA-17 (mature, minimum age 17).

- The 3DO Interactive Multiplayer is released with a price of $699.

The Modern Age: 1994–present

1994:

- *GamePro* becomes the first video game magazine to sell 500,000 copies of a single issue (January).

- Commodore files for bankruptcy.

- Sony releases the PlayStation in Japan. CD-based games become the norm.

- Sega releases the Saturn in Japan while Sega of America releases the 32X, another add-on for the Genesis.

- In Tokyo, Nintendo announces the Virtual Boy, a new video game system that uses a special virtual reality headset to display 3D red images on a black background. It uses six AA batteries for seven hours of gameplay. It will be later released in the United States for $179.95, where it will be a commercial failure.

- Apple Computer announces the Pippin video game system, based on the Macintosh personal computer. The system will later be adopted by Bandai Digital Entertainment for its own @World entertainment system but it will go completely unnoticed when officially released in 1996.

- In Japan, Nintendo and St. Giga television announce the Satellaview service, allowing Super Famicom users to download games via cable service starting from April 1995.

1995:

- Activision releases its Atari 2600 *Action Pak Volume 1* for Windows-based personal computers. Nostalgic-emulated retrogaming begins.

- Nintendo of America announces its Ultra 64 game machine. It is going to become the Nintendo 64.

- Sega Saturn is released in the United States at $349.

- The first Electronic Entertainment Expo (E3) is held in Los Angeles. Three hundred and fifty game companies show 1,300 games for video game systems and personal computers.

- The PlayStation is introduced in the United States and Europe. Price is set at $299.

1996:

- Nintendo releases the Nintendo 64 worldwide and the Game Boy Pocket portable game system in the United States.

- Capcom releases *Resident Evil*, spawning a new series of survival/horror-themed games.

- Eidos releases *Tomb Raider*, imposing the 3D third-person adventure gameplay to the attention of the general public.

- DigiPen Institute of Technology starts offering B.S. degrees in Real Time Interactive Simulation—the world's first bachelor degree program dedicated to computer and video game development.

1997:

- In Japan, Sony begins selling the Net Yaroze, a programmable PlayStation video game system.

- Sega launches the Saturn NetLink, allowing the Saturn system to connect to the Internet.

- Sony releases the Dual Analog controller for the PlayStation in the United States. The Dual Shock controller will follow one year later.

- Sony releases *Parappa the Rapper*, popularizing music/rhythm-based games.

1998:

◘ Hasbro buys Atari's home video game assets.

◘ Nintendo releases the Game Boy Color handheld video game system while also releasing camera and printer accessories for its handhelds.

◘ SNK releases the NeoGeo Pocket handheld video game system in Japan.

◘ Sega launches the Dreamcast in Japan while also holding a Gamer's Day in San Francisco. Worldwide release will follow one year later. The Dreamcast is the first system with a built-in modem for online play.

1999:

◘ Sony Computer Entertainment introduces the PocketStation handheld video game system in Japan. Games are downloaded from the PlayStation in a new format. Price is about $25.

◘ In Tokyo, Japan, Sony unveils the specifications of its next PlayStation video game system to 1500 invited guests. Nintendo soon announces its next generation console too, codenamed Dolphin.

◘ In Weirs Beach, New Hampshire, Billy Mitchell plays a "perfect" game of the arcade game *Pac-Man* in over six hours. It's the highest score that the game allows—3,333,360—and it can only be accomplished by guiding Pac-Man to eat every dot, fruit, and ghost in all 256 levels.

2000:

◘ Sony releases the PlayStation 2, the first console to have built-in DVD capabilities.

◘ At the Game Developers' Conference in San Jose, California, Bill Gates announces plans for Microsoft's Xbox video game console.

◘ Sega launches the SegaNet online gaming network. Dreamcast players can play against other players via the dial-up network. Price is $21.95 per month.

◘ At the Media Art Festival in Japan, the local Agency of Cultural Affairs proclaims the video game *Dragon Quest VII*, published by Enix for the PlayStation, as the best work of interactive digital art.

2001:

◘ Sega announces that it will halt production of the Dreamcast and shift its focus to developing software for other consoles and handheld devices.

◘ Nintendo releases the Game Boy Advance and the GameCube. Prices will be $99.99 and $199.95, respectively.

◘ Microsoft releases the Xbox, the first major console to use a hard disk and to effectively popularize online gaming. Launch price is set at $299.

◘ Sony ships a limited number of Linux kits for the PlayStation 2 in Japan. The kit includes a 40 GB hard drive, keyboard, mouse, VGA and Ethernet adapters, plus a DVD with Red Hat-based Linux OS. Price is 25,000 ¥. All 2,000 units sell out in under eight minutes.

◘ SNK of Japan shuts down the company. The company was best known for its NeoGeo arcade and home games.

◘ IBM, Toshiba, and Sony announce an agreement to develop a new computer chip, codenamed Cell, likely to be the heart of the next Sony video game system.

2002:

◘ Microsoft officially launches the Xbox Live online gaming service in the United States. The service will be available in Europe one year later.

2003:

◘ Nintendo releases the Game Boy Advance SP while it manufactures the last Famicom system.

◘ 3DO announces it has filed for Chapter 11 bankruptcy protection in the United States.

- Sony introduces the EyeToy camera for the PlayStation 2.

- Nokia tries to merge a cell phone and a handheld gaming system and releases the N-Gage. Price in the United States is $300.

2004:

- Sony releases the Universal Media Disc (UMD)-based PlayStation Portable handheld system in Japan (North American release in 2005 for $249.99), plus a slimmer version of the PlayStation 2.

- Nintendo releases its Nintendo DS dual screen handheld, which can also play Game Boy Advance titles thanks to a special cartridge slot, and announces a new console codenamed Revolution.

- Blizzard Entertainment releases *World of Warcraft*, which soon becomes the most well-known MMO game with millions of active users.

2005:

- Microsoft releases the Xbox 360 with 18 launch titles. Prices start at $299.99.

- At the Tokyo Game Show, Nintendo shows a prototype wireless controller for its upcoming Revolution video game system. It is shaped like a television remote controller and it interacts with sensors placed next to the television to detect movement.

2006:

- Nintendo renames its new Revolution console the Wii and releases it worldwide. Launch price is $249.99. The Wii will redefine the concept of playing video games thanks to its easy-to-use motion-based controls.

- Sony releases the Blu-Ray–enabled Playstation 3. Prices start at $499. Release in Europe and Australia will follow in 2007.

- Nintendo releases the DS Lite, a slimmer DS, with instant success.

2008:

◘   Nintendo launches the Wii Fit exercise game for its Wii console. Price is $90 and it includes a balance board input device that can also be used by other games.

◘   Nintendo releases the DSi, a new DS with a larger screen and a camera but without the Game Boy Advance slot.

2009:

◘   Sony releases the PSP Go, removing UMD disk-based games in favor of digital downloads. Also, a new, slimmer version of the PS3 is released.

◘   Nintendo announces that total shipments of its DS portable consoles have topped 100 million worldwide.

2010:

◘   Nintendo reveals a new handheld system, the 3DS, which is able to offer a 3D experience without the need of special glasses.

◘   Microsoft introduces a new slimmer and more reliable version of the Xbox 360.

◘   Sony and Microsoft release their respective motion controlling devices, Move and Kinect.

◘   Panasonic announces its intention to get into the handheld gaming market with the Jungle, a system designed to bring MMO games on the go.

Part I

From research labs and academia to the
birth and booming of a new industry

The Beginning
• • • • • • • • • •

The first general-purpose electronic computer is considered to be the Electronic and Numerical Integrator and Computer (ENIAC), developed secretly in the United States during World War II to compute artillery firing tables and manipulate complex data related to the hydrogen bomb. The huge system was made public in 1946 and, obviously, no one even thought of using it to play games.

Nonetheless, the time of video and computer games was approaching fast and, in 1947, the first known electronic game played on a screen was developed. The cathode ray tube (CRT) was a technology perfected in the thirties, and, by the mid-forties, it was the main building block in all TV systems. It shouldn't be surprising then that the first game using this technology, named the Cathode Ray Tube Amusement Device, was developed at DuMont Laboratories, a well-known television manufacturer.

The ENIAC at work.

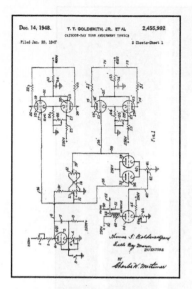
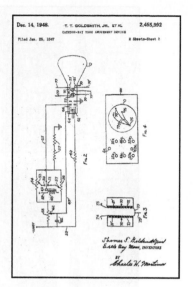

First two pages of the patent filed for the CRT Amusement Device, the first electronic game ever to be played on a screen.

The main author of the project was Dr. Thomas Goldsmith Jr. (1910–2009) who, together with Estle Ray Man, devised a clever system of manipulating the electron beam by controlling a set of variable resistors to simulate a simple missile shooting game. Only a dot was displayed on the screen but different targets were graphically represented by transparent layers applied on the CRT's screen to simulate a radar-like environment. The project was successfully filed in a patent but, regrettably, DuMont didn't pursue this research further.

In 1950, the first computer game was designed by famous mathematician and engineer Claude Shannon (1916–2001) in the seminal paper "Programming a Computer for Playing Chess."[1] Unfortunately, though, no computers at the time were powerful enough to implement a chess game so his design was not transformed into an actual program.

The first actual game programmed on a computer was in 1952 when Ph.D. candidate Alexander Douglas (born 1921) from the University of Cambridge, UK, developed a tic-tac-toe game named *Noughts and Crosses*. His game, also called *OXO*, was a part of his thesis on human and computer interaction. The game ran on the Electronic Delay Storage Automatic Calculator (EDSAC), which was the first machine programmable by means of assembly instructions, as opposed to turning switches or connecting cables as required on the ENIAC or earlier computers.

---

[1] Published in *Philosophical Magazine*, 7th series, Vol. 41, No. 314 (March 1950): pp. 256–275.

The vacuum tube-based EDSAC, the first computer to ever run a game.

Playing *OXO* involved inputting moves into a rotating phone dial and the nine-cell board could be viewed through a tiny 35 × 16 pixel display. However, the EDSAC was a one-of-a-kind machine so the game never had the chance to be appreciated outside of Cambridge University.

There were a few more artificial intelligence (AI) research projects within academia that related to board and mathematical games such as checkers and nim, but let's shift our attention again to the US East Coast where the first two-player sport-inspired video game, designed for mere entertainment, was born: *Tennis for Two*.

In 1958, William Higinbotham (1910–1994), a physicist working at the Brookhaven National Laboratories in New York, decided to "spice up" the annual open house event by giving the visitors a game to play. He did this by using an analog system able to compute missile trajectories and applied it to simulate a much friendlier tennis ball. The computer displayed the game by using a small oscilloscope, and the game could be played by using two controllers featuring a button to change the ball direction and a knob to affect the rebounding angle (see the figure on the opposite page). These controllers were provided to visitors who wanted to try the new technological marvel. Hundreds of people queued up to play the game that was showcased again a year later through a bigger oscilloscope.

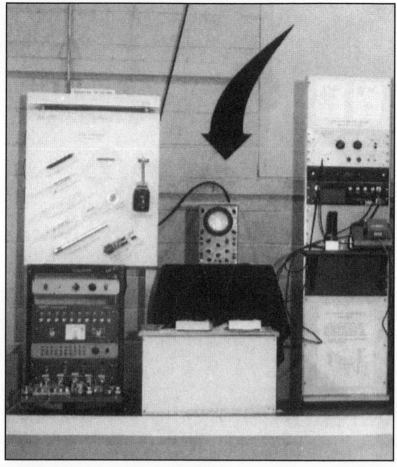

The computer running *Tennis for Two*. The arrow points at the oscilloscope showing the ball being bounced around by the players thanks to the provided controllers (the two white boxes on the table right below the oscilloscope).

Like *OXO* before it, though, *Tennis for Two* was created in a laboratory, restricting its use to that particular environment where it was produced and making it difficult for the game to become widely known and enjoyed.

The first time a video game was finally able to attract people's attention on a daily basis was in 1962 at the prestigious Massachusetts Institute of Technology (MIT) in Cambridge, Massachusetts. This video game was played using a state-of-the-art computer that the electrical engineering department of the university received in 1961. This computer was called the Programmed Data Processor 1, or PDP-1. It was a mainframe sporting 9 KB of memory and a monitor (see the figure on the top of page 6).

The PDP-1 by Digital Equipment Corporation (DEC). It used punched paper tapes as its primary storage medium and instructions had to be input through a tape reader.

Among those allowed to access the machine were a group of students from the Tech Model Railroad Club (TMRC). The TMRC loved experimenting with new technologies, so they were very excited by the newly arrived "toy" and decided to build a test application to push it to the limits. This small group of friends, led by Stephen Russell (born 1931), developed *Spacewar!*, a combat-style game in which two players had to face each other in a space shootout while avoiding the gravity well of a star placed in the middle of the screen.

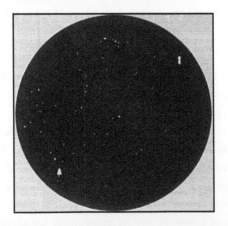

A close up on the PDP-1 monitor running *Spacewar!*.

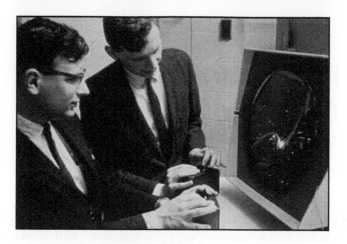

A *Spacewar!* match in action.

In the following years, different versions of the game were developed, featuring improvements such as better physics, real star constellations as a backdrop, and a pair of button-based remote controls, made by team members Alan Kotok and Bob Sanders. Thanks to these improvements, *Spacewar!* quickly became so well known that DEC started shipping it with the machines as a demo/test program. It was so popular, in fact, that when a US university purchased a PDP (for about $120,000), it was the first application that students loaded and played when the computer was free from more serious and academically-inclined duties.

Overall, 50 PDP-1 units were produced and the last working unit is still show-cased at the Computer History Museum[2] where visitors can admire *Spacewar!* in all of its original glory.

---

[2] For more information, see http://pdp-1.computerhistory.org/.

The First Commercial Game
and the First Home Console

● ● ● ● ● ● ● ● ● ● ● ● ● ● ● ● ●

Among the people who played *Spacewar!* was Nolan Bushnell (born 1943), an engineering student at the University of Utah in the mid-sixties. Bushnell was a natural-born businessman with innovative ideas and a passion for games so he understood right away that video games had potential from a commercial perspective. In 1969, while working for a company named Ampex, he joined forces with his friend and colleague Ted Dabney (born 1937) to start turning his vision into reality.

The very first idea was to use a $4,000 microcomputer, a DEC PDP-8, to design a coin-operated system able to play a few different games. Another friend, Larry Bryant, was supposed to take care of the actual programming and each of them

A young Ted Dabney (left) with Nolan Bushnell, the founding fathers of the video game industry.

agreed to provide $100 to fund the new venture. While Dabney and Bushnell quickly did so, Bryant never contributed his share and, since it didn't take long to realize the expensive computer would have made the project economically unfeasible, the development took a different direction without Larry's involvement.

The duo worked from home in a small lab obtained by converting the room of Ted's daughter, Terri, over to a work area. Ted started designing a circuit that didn't need a computer but used transistor to transistor logic (TTL) components instead to keep costs down as much as possible. A cheap black-and-white TV set was used as display and no central processing unit (CPU) was included in the board design since the early ones produced at the time were much too expensive. The first outcome was a technical demo able to move simple squared images on a TV screen. From there, the prototype developed into a clever single-player version of *Spacewar!*, aptly named *Computer Space*.

In *Computer Space*, the player handled a rocket ship and had to destroy a computer-controlled saucer. There were no "lives" in the traditional game sense; instead, the gaming session had a fixed length of 100 seconds. Once time was up, the player would see how many times he successfully hit the saucer and whether or not he scored more hits than the computer did.

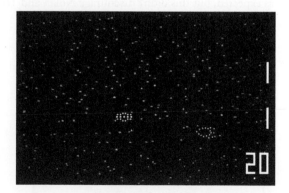

Computer Space,[3] the first commercial coin-operated game ever produced (Nutting Associates, 1971).

Besides the simple scoring mechanic, the game also had a special visual effect twist. If the vendor wanted to, he or she could extend the playing time by another 99 seconds thanks to a special mode that Ted called "Hyperspace" where the video switched from white-on-black to black-on-white, adding some variety and excitement to the overall experience.

After the prototype was ready, Nolan and Ted had to find someone to mass-produce and sell it. These responsibilities fell to Nutting Associates, a struggling

---

[3] A modern PC rendition of *Computer Space*, together with *SpaceWar!*, *Tennis for Two*, and *OXO*, can be played at www.computerspacefan.com.

company that was looking for some fresh ideas and was more than happy to give this new technological marvel a try. The deal was soon sealed with Nutting agreeing to produce and distribute the game while allowing Nolan and Ted to retain ownership of the intellectual property rights and paying them a royalty on each cabinet sold.

The creation of the first commercial video game was now officially in progress. Having worked in amusement parks during his youth, Bushnell felt strongly that the game's cabinet was also an important factor in attracting potential players so he designed a shiny, futuristic case in fiberglass that was sure to do the trick. The first of these cabinets was placed at a pub named the Dutch Goose, next to Stanford University, as a testing experiment. This trial was actually quite successful, pushing Nutting to produce 1,500 cabinets and to plan for a version enabling two-player action at a higher price.

There was something Nolan overlooked, though—the Dutch Goose was a hangout for Stanford students and Stanford University had a PDP-1. Many of the players in the Dutch Goose had also played *Spacewar!* and had no problem understanding the game. However, this wasn't true for the average person who found one of the 1,500 cabinets in a pub around the country. In the end, most people probably just stared at the oddly shaped cabinet in awe, but ultimately shied away. *Computer Space* didn't fare as well as expected, but this didn't discourage Nolan and Ted.

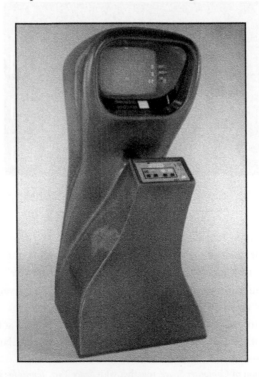

Computer Space's futuristic cabinet, designed by Nolan Bushnell to attract as much attention as possible.

Ralph Baer, the man behind the first home video gaming system.

While Bushnell and Dabney were trying to bring video games into pubs, another talented engineer named Ralph Baer (born 1922) worked to bring them straight into people's homes. Ralph Baer was born in Germany to a Jewish family and had to leave school at an early age due to the ethnic discrimination of the Nazi regime in the thirties. Luckily, his family escaped to New York before things got worse. Once there, he learned electronics through a correspondence course and only after World War II could he properly complete his formal education.

On September 1, 1966, while on the bus, Baer started writing out some simple notes detailing a system for playing games on a TV. He had the very same idea previously in 1951 while he was working for a small TV manufacturer, but at the time it didn't interest his boss and he wasn't allowed to proceed further. But things were different in 1966. Baer was now a bright Division Manager for Sanders Associates, a research and development (R&D) company doing mainly research and contract work for the US Army, and it was relatively easy for him to convince his directors to allocate a small fund for a research project based on his new idea.

The project started in early 1967 and, by November 11, there was a prototype for a two-player ping-pong game. The system was perfected further in the following months and nicknamed the "Brown Box," which also featured a light gun device that was able to shoot white dots on the screen (see the figure at the top of page 12). This was actually the feature that excited Baer's boss the most and allowed Baer to keep the whole project alive despite the skepticism of other senior executives.

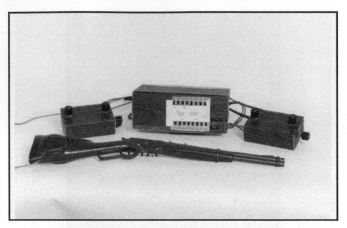

The Brown Box prototype with the light gun add-on.

Playing table tennis on the Odyssey.

Once the Brown Box was ready, it was time to look for a manufacturer/distributor. After a few failed discussions, TV manufacturer Magnavox sealed the deal and, finally, in May 1972, the Odyssey Home Entertainment System was sent to Magnavox retailers.

The Odyssey was an analog machine able to display one line and three small white squares across the screen; it had no sound capabilities. The machine came with a set of cartridges that switched circuits inside the main console to alter the behavior and placement of the graphical element on the screen. The default game, named "table tennis," showed a line dividing the screen into two equal parts. Players controlled one square each by moving it up/down and left/right using two independent paddles on the sides of the controller. The goal of the game was to bounce the third square back and forth to each other (see the figure at the bottom of the opposite page). There was no onscreen score display.

The other games, which were started by inserting specific cartridges, were made more interesting and meaningful by applying an overlay to visualize additional colors, boards, paths, and targets.

Overlay for the game *Haunted House,* where two players had to hide and chase each other around an old manor by playing cards to decide in which spot to move.

The Odyssey was a truly revolutionary device that used the table tennis game both as a stand-alone game and also as a tool for successfully bringing several board and table game concepts onto the TV screen, with the video experience enhanced by also using dice, cards, chips, etc. Unfortunately, Magnavox used a doubtful marketing approach that alienated many potential costumers; not only was the original price set at $100, which was very high for the time,[4] but the Odyssey was also proposed as an add-on for their own television sets. In the end, many people using different TV brands were misled into thinking they couldn't use the Odyssey and missed out on the opportunity of experiencing the very first home video games. In 1972, about 100,000 units were sold, and when the system was discontinued in 1975, up to 350,000 units and 80,000 light guns had been shipped.

---

[4] Baer's original idea was to sell the device for as little as $19.95!

Atari, *Pong*, and the Jackals

The less than spectacular debut of *Computer Space* didn't discourage Nolan Bushnell and Ted Dabney. In fact, Nolan was ready to pitch some new ideas to Bally, one of the most important pinball and slot machine manufacturers of the time, but the big company wasn't keen to deal with the two men as long as they were in business with Nutting. For Ted and Nolan, it was the right time to leave the struggling company and start a new, real business on their own.

So far, the duo unofficially called their venture "Syzygy," meaning an alignment of celestial bodies.[5] However, having the name legally approved was not as straightforward as they expected. Ted remembers: "When we tried to incorporate under Syzygy, the office of the California Secretary of State said it was already taken and asked us to submit three alternatives. We submitted 'Hane,' 'Sente,' and 'Atari.'[6] The state selected 'Atari' for us."

The two friends provided initial funding of $250 dollars each to start Atari in 1972 and the first employee they hired was Cynthia Villanueva, a 17-year-old girl who used to babysit Bushnell's kids. Her duties as a secretary included answering phone calls and making people wait in order to simulate a very busy and professional environment.

It was time for some new projects, and a contract was signed with Bally to deliver a new game. Having understood that *Computer Space* was too complex for the average person, Bushnell's next idea was to develop a simple sport-based game. The first option was a driving game, but after having witnessed the upcoming Odyssey console, the idea of an improved ping-pong game started shaping up. Ultimately, Nolan assigned a pet project to a newly hired engineer, Allan Alcorn, with the idea of getting him accustomed to the original motion circuit that Ted designed for *Computer Space*. After that, Allan would be able to move to more serious and difficult projects.[7]

Starting from Ted's original design, Allan began crafting a new TTL circuit and enhanced the ping-pong game concept by adding some of his own ideas. For example,

---

[5] The name was proposed by Larry Bryant during the very early days of their partnership.

[6] Hane, Sente, and Atari are all words from the Japanese game *Go*, which Nolan and Ted enjoyed playing in their spare time.

[7] In reality, to keep Allan motivated, Nolan told him he was going to develop a very important game for a newly signed contract with General Electric.

The original *Pong* prototype.

the paddles were built by different segments, which affected the ball's rebounding angle, and the ball speed was set to increase during long rallies. The prototype for this game (named *Pong*) was constructed of a handmade cabinet (put together by Ted) including a $75 dollar black-and-white TV set and a slot to insert coins. During September 1972, *Pong* was placed on a barrel in a bar named Andy Capps in Sunnyvale, California, for testing purposes (like *Computer Space* at the Dutch Goose months earlier).

Andy Capps had a relatively big room at the back where a few pinball machines, a jukebox, and a *Computer Space* cabinet were located for the customers' enjoyment. In short, Andy Capps was itself the prototype of what would soon become the very successful video game arcade that started spawning all over the world in a matter of only a few years.

About two weeks after the installation of the machine, the owner of Andy Capps called Allan because the game had stopped working. Once the engineer arrived, he realized with great surprise that the failure was due to coins overflowing out of the little box! The game was so popular that customers even started to queue up in front of the bar before opening time and, once in, they rushed to play *Pong* without ordering any drinks, leaving the bar owner completely puzzled.

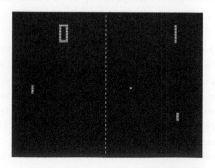

A screenshot from the original *Pong*.

The success in the small tavern was phenomenal and Atari was finally ready to send its first product to Bally, which had already paid $24,000 and owned the rights to it according to their original agreement. Surprisingly, though, bringing the deal to a happy conclusion was not easy. Ted recalls the events that followed during those days:

> We built 12 Pong games on our own. We sent one of these to Bally. Bushnell went to Chicago several times to get Bally to accept it, with no success. We then put 10 of these games out in several locations. The results were outrageous. We put an income report together to send to Bally. The numbers were so big that I decided to submit only one third of the numbers. They still thought that we exaggerated the report!

Despite Atari's efforts, Bally didn't realize the potential of the product and decided to cancel the agreement, leaving Atari on its own with *Pong.*

Atari now had a sure success in its hands but was left without the support of an established partner. Those were definitely the most critical days for the young startup since raising interest and money wasn't easy. "People would look at you like you had three heads: 'You mean you are going to put a TV in a box with a coin slot and play games on it?'" recalls Nolan. Others were ready to bet vandals would simply break all the cabinets to steal the TVs inside.

Ted still remembers the situation very clearly:

> After we left Nutting, Nolan and I had some royalties coming in on Computer Space. All of this money was needed to set up our office and pay the rent. We both lived on the coins we made from our street operations. After we got the contract from Bally, all of the royalties and the money from Bally were still used for the facilities, but now we also had to pay Allan and Cynthia and pay for the first 12 games we built. Nolan and I still took no salary. After Bally's rejection we still had very little money. Nolan and I were doing much better with the income from the 10 Pongs that we put out. Cash was still quite scarce when we decided to build the first 50 production units, so I used my own money to buy the Hitachi TVs. When I ordered the cabinets I told the guy that I may not be able to pay him. His response was, "We'll deliver them. What's your address?"

In the end, selling the games and securing even a small loan required the joint effort and perseverance of both Ted and Nolan:

> When we started to build the first 50 *Pongs,* Nolan was standing up near the front of the shop watching what was going on. I went up to him and told him his job now was to sell these things. His smile went to a frown very quickly. He sauntered off to his office in kind of a hangdog manner. He came back about an hour later looking very perplexed. He said, "I just sold 300 games. 50 to one guy, 100 to another, and Bob Portale gave me an order for 150." It was pretty clear that we were in for the ride of our lives. Shortly after that, we found a roller ring and started moving production there.
>
> Nolan knew we were going to need more money. I don't know how he did it but he got Portale, the owner of a major distribution company of coin-op and vending machines

in the Los Angeles area, to give him a purchase order for the 150 units. The coin-op industry had never worked with purchase orders before. He wanted this to show the bank so we could get a loan. We figured that $3,000 would do.

I contacted Gary Teasdale, who was the manager of the Wells Fargo in Cupertino where I had my accounts. He said that Nolan and I had to come in to talk with him. On the way over, Nolan said that I should let him do the talking because he could make it sound very good. I told Nolan that the bank had no upside on this. He needed to know about the downside. Nolan said "Don't worry about it. I know what I'm doing." So I said "Okay" and Nolan did the talking.

I called Teasdale about two days later and he said he didn't want to give us the loan. I went straight over and had a long talk with him. We got the money.

The new credit allowed Atari to start its own plant to manufacture and market *Pong* in late 1972 with a huge, immediate success.

Interestingly, even though the industry just started and there were very few people involved in it, problems were already approaching. *Pong*'s resemblance to Odyssey's own "table tennis" didn't pass unnoticed; it was proven that Bushnell visited a Magnavox booth in 1972 where the Odyssey was promoted and he played with it, so Magnavox accused Atari of copying its product and infringing on the related patents, including the underlying technology.

Atari's lawyer suggested they would win in court since Dabney originally succeeded in controlling objects on a screen in a completely autonomous and independent way. The two games were also quite different both in architecture and gameplay;

The original leaflet advertising *Pong.*

for example, the Odyssey didn't use integrated circuits, and the game had no score and no sound. Further, the paddles in the Odyssey game could also move left and right and the system used a third knob to change the ball trajectory with a sort of "after touch," or "English" effect, while in *Pong* the speed of the ball and its rebounding angles were determined according to rally length and hitting position.

Regardless of the possible court outcome, though, the legal costs involved in contesting the claims would have been more than those even a successful startup like Atari could have afforded at the time, so Bushnell opted for an out-of-court settlement with Magnavox, which was finally agreed upon in 1976 with Atari paying $700,000 to become an official Magnavox licensee.

Magnavox wasn't the only company that noticed the new *Pong* phenomenon. As people realized the potential of the new technology, dozens of imitators started cropping up all over, not only in the United States but also abroad where the machine was soon exported. Bushnell called these imitators "Jackals" and decided to fight back—not by legal means (Magnavox was already taking care of that by suing anyone with a game similar to theirs), but by constantly proposing new games to remain ahead of the competition.

At first, Atari started creating its own *Pong* clones with games such as *Pin Pong*, *Dr. Pong*, *QuadraPong*, and more, but soon they started to produce new and innovative concepts as well, such as *Gotcha* (below) and *Gran Track 10* (opposite page). There was more work to do to outflank the competition effectively and maintain the biggest share of the market.

Original flyer for *Gotcha* (1973), the first maze-chase game and the first game to spur some controversy in the media and among players—the controllers were pink rubber bulges that somewhat resembled female anatomy and had to be squeezed to play. The bulges were replaced with more "standard" joysticks in later editions of the game.

Gran Track 10 (1974) was the first racing game and the first game to use ROM chips to store graphic data that went beyond simple lines and squares. Despite a simple top-down view, it used realistic controls such as a steering wheel, gears, and pedals, delivering a new and immersive experience.

At that time, distributors tried to "play fair" with each other; if distributor X and distributor Y were both operating in a common area, they would market products from different brands. This "fairness" forced exclusive agreements even when the clients didn't want them, and it meant that Atari would only be able to sell its games to one distributor per region while all the other distributors had no choice but to pick up the competition. To work around this stalemate, Bushnell had the idea of competing with himself and mischievously started another company, Kee Games, in 1973.

Kee Games was managed by Bushnell's neighbor and long time friend Joe Keenan with the main purpose of shamelessly spawning clones of Atari games to reach other distributors and effectively increase Atari's market share. Kee Games hired a couple of Atari's top people, such as Steve Bristow; while in public Atari and Kee were fierce enemies, in reality, Bushnell and Allan Alcorn were on Kee Games' Board of Directors and indirectly controlled the subsidiary company. In addition to producing Atari clones like *Elimination* (a copy of *QuadraPong*) or *Formula K* (a copy of *Gran Track 10*), Kee Games soon started shining from its own light thanks to Joe's bright guidance and an original hit by Steve. This original title, *Tank*, was released in 1974.

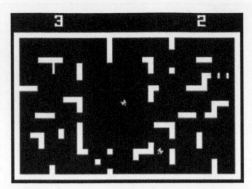

Tank, the biggest hit in arcades in 1974, by Kee Games. Like Atari's *Gran Track 10*, it used ROM for displaying better graphics.

Bushnell's trick was discovered in December 1974, forcing the two companies to merge officially. Joe became Atari's President, since he proved to be very successful with Kee Games, while Bushnell decided to limit his direct control to the engineering side. As an official subsidiary, Kee Games kept producing games for Atari until 1978.

Pong Goes Home
• • • • • • • • • • •

Having affirmed its presence in the arcade scene, it was time for Atari to grow in a different direction and to bring its most popular game, *Pong*, into homes.

The *Home Pong* project, originally codenamed Darlene after an attractive employee (the atmosphere at Atari was extremely casual at the time), was assigned to Allan Alcorn and Harold Lee. The duo had a first working prototype in the fall of 1974, but finding a company interested in distributing and selling it wasn't as straightforward as it should have been after *Pong*'s original success. Most retailers were still doubtful about the prospects of video games and thought that people, while enjoying them at the pub, wouldn't really want to play such things at home.

Only Sears Roebuck & Co., the biggest department store chain of the time, showed some interest. However, it was not the consumer electronics section that was interested, but the sports department—they thought a sporting game would make a good addition to their winter catalogue during a time of the year when they usually sold only hockey equipment. Despite some minor hiccups (the *Pong* prototype didn't work at the live demo arranged in Sears headquarters due to a signal interference, and Alcorn had to fix it on the fly), the deal went through and Sears ordered 150,000 units for the 1975 holiday season. Atari couldn't fulfill such a huge order on its own, so it had to rely on external investors. In particular, a very famous venture capitalist named Don Valentine helped Atari grow further and acquire more manufacturing facilities. Atari's *Home Pong*, named *Tele-Games* by Sears, was a big hit and all 150,000 units were sold during the 1975 Christmas season and in early 1976.

The original *Home Pong* by Atari distributed under Sears's *Tele-Games* brand.

As with the original *Pong*, the Jackals didn't wait long before trying to get a share of the new home video gaming market. More than 70 companies all around the world, from electronics giants like Philips to domestic kitchen appliance manufacturers like Italian Zanussi, developed their own version of the game (see the figure below).

While most of these companies soon faded away without leaving any meaningful trace, two of them would actually write important pages in the history of video games. These Jackals were Coleco and Nintendo.

Coleco, the Connecticut Leather Company, was founded in 1932 by Maurice Greenberg. Throughout the years, it gradually shifted its focus from manufacturing leather goods to toys and, ultimately, to electronic games. In 1976, it produced the *Telstar*, a *Pong* clone that was highly successful during that year (see the figure on the opposite page). This first experiment was followed by the development of several dedicated electronic consoles that ultimately led to the ColecoVision system.

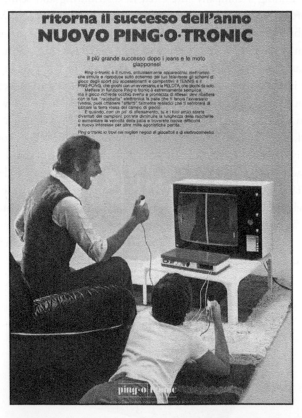

An Italian ad page for the very rare "Ping-O-Tronic" console by Zanussi. The ad says: "The new Ping-O-Tronic: the biggest success after jeans and Japanese motorbikes." The system also featured a light gun add-on like the original Odyssey. *Pong* clones were popping up all around the world.

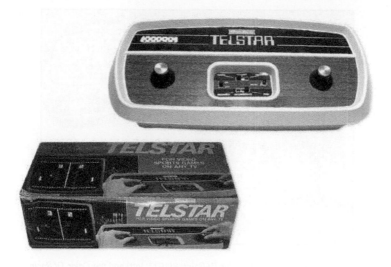

Coleco's *Telstar,* the best-selling Home Pong game in 1976. The main ad line on the box stressed "For Video Sports Games on any TV," avoiding any possible misunderstanding like those that plagued Odyssey's marketing by Magnavox.

Nintendo, on the other hand, was founded in 1886 by Fusajiro Yamauchi under the name Marufuku Company to produce "hanafuda," a typical set of Japanese playing cards still manufactured today. In 1951, the name was changed to Nintendo and, due to struggling economic conditions, the company started trying different ventures as varied as running a taxi service, a TV network, and even a chain of hotels before ultimately returning to games.

Around the same time, thanks to an agreement with a growing company in the local amusement machine manufacturing business named Nakamura Manufacturing Company (later renamed Namco), Atari's coin-ops started getting properly distributed in Japan. It didn't take long for the new form of entertainment to develop a huge following among Japanese youngsters, and suddenly electronic games started to attract the interest of many different companies in the Far East.

In its search for new ventures, Nintendo decided to jump head-on into the new market. They first licensed the table tennis concept from Magnavox, and then started developing their own systems. The first console was named *Color TV Game 6* and was launched in Japan in 1977. In the following years, more models were released, including a *Color TV Game 15*, a driving game named *Color TV Racing 112* (see the figure on page 24),[8] and a porting of Nintendo's arcade version of Atari's breakout arcade hit, *Burokku kuzushi*.

---

[8] The casings for *Racing 112* and *Burukku kuzushi* were the first projects assigned to a newly hired designer, Shigeru Miyamoto, who soon became an inspiring figure in the video game industry.

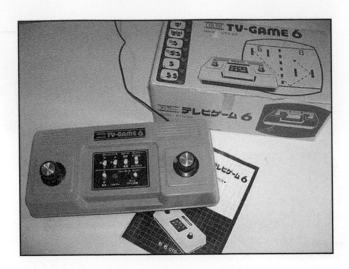

Nintendo's first video game consoles, the *Color TV Game 6* (1977, left) and the *Color TV Racing 112* (1978, right).

Once again, Atari tried to remain ahead of the competition and started design-ing its own *Home Pong* variations. However, the market soon stagnated because, de-spite minor modifications to the games, people grew tired of always playing the same ones. Something more was needed, and a new generation of home console was loom-ing ahead.

Home Consoles

• • • • • • • • • • •

All dedicated video game systems, no matter how successful at launch, had a short life span. To grow further, the industry needed a new type of console—a type that was able to play games that could be loaded by the users like computer programs. Luckily, it didn't take long for the first models to arrive.

Bushnell understood the public need perfectly. In 1976, he pushed Atari to work on a project codenamed Stella (this time the name wasn't derived from a pretty employee but from the bicycle that one of the engineers used to ride to work). Stella would have had an unimaginable impact on the burgeoning game industry, but before it was released, other companies came up with their own innovative consoles.

Fairchild Channel F and RCA Studio II

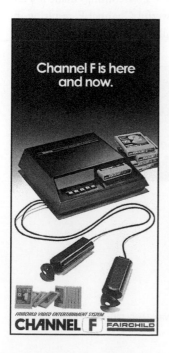

Fairchild Semiconductors was the first to release a home console that, besides having a built-in *Home Pong* game, was also able to play games stored in dedicated cartridges sold separately. The system was first named Video Entertainment System (VES) but was soon renamed Channel F and featured Fairchild's own F8 CPU, an 8-bit processor running at 2 MHz. The console could display color graphics (eight colors), and sported a built-in speaker and two original controllers that were able to function both as a four-way joystick and as a paddle to be twisted/rotated clockwise or counterclockwise. Overall, it had 26 cartridges (named Videocarts) featuring mostly educational games targeted at young children (see the figure on the top of page 26). The console sold for $169.95 and the cartridges sold separately at $19.95 each.

Original ad for the Fairchild Channel F, the first home computer cartridge-based system released in August 1976.

One of the Channel F original Videocarts.

Another system was released in January 1977, the Studio II. Its manufacturer was RCA, which, after having rejected the Odyssey years earlier, tried to acquire a significant spot in the new business. Like Fairchild, RCA decided to use a proprietary 8-bit microprocessor, the RCA 1802. The console came with five simple games pre-installed and it could also accommodate dedicated cartridges.

Unfortunately, the Studio II lacked proper controllers and relied on numeric keypads instead. It also had very limited audio capabilities (just a simple buzzer sound) and the graphics were only black and white. These shortcomings made it a far less attractive item for most players than the more powerful Channel F, resulting in very little commercial success and only 11 games actually produced.

The RCA Studio II. Originally retailing at $149 in January 1977, it was a very rare console that was soon forgotten.

In any case, neither of these consoles had enough time to build an audience because the flood of *Pong* clones temporarily decreased the general public's interest in video games. At the same time, a new star was already shining on the horizon.

The VCS Emerges amidst Big Changes at Atari

In 1976, under Alcorn's leadership, the research on Stella was well underway and progress was steady. Atari engineers had seen the Channel F and they were able to fine tune their ideas, targeting a more powerful machine from the ground up. The system was built around a MOS 6507 CPU, a cheaper version of the 6502 model[9] but still allowing much more flexibility than Fairchild's F8.

Stella was officially renamed the Video Computer System (VCS) as launch approached. However, Atari needed more funding before proceeding with the actual production and manufacturing stages. After evaluating a few different options, Bushnell decided to sell Atari to Warner Communications for $28 million in October 1976. The new owner immediately invested about $100 million in the company while maintaining its upper management structure, including Nolan and Joe Keenan, intact. It seemed all problems were solved forever, but that sense of security was short-lived.

The VCS was officially released in October 1977 with nine launch titles (see the figure at the top of page 28). The console came bundled with *Combat* (see the second figure on page 28), a game clearly inspired by earlier Kee Games' success *Tank*, and Atari optimistically manufactured 400,000 consoles. Unfortunately, shipping problems and a temporary shift in consumer interest from home consoles to the new handheld electronic games by Mattel and Coleco resulted in sales throughout 1978 proceeding at a steady but disappointing pace.

Steve Ross (1927–1992), Warner's owner, was deeply disappointed by the 1977 holiday season and slow start in 1978. He was so disappointed, in fact, that he even considered the possibility of liquidating the company. In February 1978, he hired Ray Kassar (born 1928), a very experienced manager and former vice president of Burlington Industries (the largest textile manufacturer in the United States), as a consultant to get a better insight into Atari's possibilities. Though Kassar knew nothing about video games, he understood the potential of the VCS and was confident that the company prospects would soon change for the better.

---

[9] Compared to the more expensive 6502, the 6507 had fewer pins for the address bus and, as a result, it could address less memory than the original model. This choice, though understandable from an economic perspective, ultimately forced games on the VCS to be simpler than those on competing machines that used a fully-fledged 6502 or another CPU able to address more memory.

The Atari VCS, later renamed 2600, was launched during October 1977 selling for $199. Both paddles and eight-direction joysticks were provided to allow different types of games.

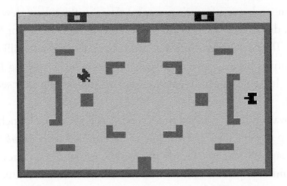

A screenshot from *Combat*, the cartridge that came bundled with the VCS.

At this time, there was some friction between the old Atari management, especially Bushnell, and the new owner. This was partly due to Kassar's intruding presence and his "traditional" working style, which clashed directly with Bushnell's "work smarter, not harder" laid back approach. For example, before Kassar's arrival, many Atari management meetings actually took place in a hot tub. It must have been a truly amusing scene to witness Ray's first visit to Atari; a Harvard graduate, he arrived impeccably dressed and driven by a chauffeured limousine while Bushnell welcomed him, wearing jeans and a t-shirt that said "I love to screw." Obviously, the differences were not only aesthetic and soon deeply contrasting ideas on how to strategize the company's next moves emerged.

The slow sales in 1978 made Bushnell believe the market was already close to being saturated and the VCS design was too constrained in memory and features. He believed that Atari should have started to focus on a new, more powerful iteration of the system in time for the 1979 holiday season. Warner management and Kassar, on the other hand, had a different appraisal of the situation; in November 1978, with the holiday season approaching, it was decided to remove Bushnell from his duties[10] and appoint Kassar as the new CEO.

Kassar's approach was to concentrate on marketing to maximize the potential of his products, whatever they were. Even though the coin-op division was much more profitable at the time (classic titles such as *Missile Command, Asteroids, Centipede, Tempest,* and others made millions in profits), the main product was considered to be the VCS, so it was there that he focused all the company's energies and resources.

Despite this new attitude, the R&D department was very active during the late seventies and early eighties[11] and Alcorn was already working on a new programmable handheld/tabletop game system codenamed Cosmos. While still offering simple 2D-based games, the Cosmos was unique in its use of holographic technology to provide exciting background images for immersing players in a completely new 3D experience. However, Kassar feared this new device might have competed with the VCS and "cannibalized" its sales so he ultimately decided to cancel the project before launch despite several thousands of pre-orders. This move upset Alcorn, who quit the company soon after.

Flyer for the never-released Atari Cosmos (1981).

---

[10] Having agreed to a seven-year non-competition clause when selling Atari to Warner, Nolan was basically outlawed from the video game business he created. However, he succeeded in working with video games again by launching Chuck E. Cheese's Pizza Time Theatre, where kids could play video games while waiting for their pizzas. He revived this idea more recently with the uWink restaurants chain and he is still an active businessman and entrepreneur.

[11] R&D for the VCS/2600 was also carried out by other companies like Cynex, which produced peripherals like the Game Mate II—the first wireless joysticks—in 1982.

Many of the original Atari employees, including both executives and developers, quit after Bushnell's departure because they didn't feel comfortable in the new environment and with the working style. In fact, the only early employee who survived was Cynthia Villanueva, the woman whom Bushnell hired at the very beginning as his secretary to make the company appear bigger and more respectable. Despite all this, Kassar's leadership and marketing-centered approach proved to be effective in the short term and the VCS became the biggest success the industry had ever seen. In 1977, Atari had $75 million in sales, which grew to more than $2 billion in less than three years.

The VCS was then renamed the 2600 after the unit's part number CX2600, when Atari was finally getting ready to launch a new, more powerful console (named 5200) towards the end of 1982. Sales for the VCS/2600 system remained very strong until the infamous video game crash of 1983, which will be extensively analyzed in Part II. By then, the installed user base was probably around 14 or 15 million. After 1983, the VCS/2600 completely lost its appeal to new gamers in North America and Europe, but, from 1986 onwards, it was still produced in a simpler and cheaper restyled version renamed Atari 2600 Jr. This "new" console was marketed in emerging countries like Brazil and across Asia where it was sold for under $50 with much success.

The smaller Atari 2600 Jr., which gave a new life to the venerable VCS from 1986 to 1991.

Ultimately, the VCS/2600 system was officially discontinued on January 1, 1992, after having sold an estimated 20 to 22 million units all around the globe. (The exact number is not known since Atari never released precise unit sales data.)[12]

Easter Eggs and the Birth of Third-Party Software

Since his very first introductory speech after becoming the new CEO of Atari, Kassar showed a lack of understanding of the people and skills needed to succeed in the video

---

[12] Once the 2600 was finally discontinued, Atari reported to have sold around 30 million consoles overall, but this number likely also included the sales of the Atari 5200, Atari 7800, and Atari XEGS (a console based on Atari's 8-bit computers), plus all of the restyled versions of the original VCS.

game industry. For example, when asked whether he felt comfortable working in such a creative environment, he replied that he was used to creative people since he had worked with towel designers all his life. This comment granted him the nickname Towel Czar.

The fractured workplace environment was not limited to Kassar, but also extended across the company between the new executives who had no understanding of or appreciation for technical/design skills, and the programmers/designers who could hardly stand to be managed by people they considered incompetent. Things only became worse when the games started bringing in huge amounts of money.

At that time, there were 12 people in charge of developing games for the console—known as the VCS consumer group—and each person was a programmer/designer in charge of a single project. They were responsible for every aspect of the game (design, programming, artwork, etc.), which took, on average, three to six months to complete. Each person in the group had a standard salary (around $25,000–$30,000 per year) and was considered to be like any other employee. Their names were not credited on their games and the company didn't plan for any performance bonus. For example, Rick Mauer, the programmer responsible for porting *Space Invaders* to the VCS, received no credit and had no extra compensation beside his standard salary, despite the more than $100 million that the game grossed in sales.

The unhappiness of the employees reached a climax in 1979. One of Atari's engineers, Warren Robinett, was working on a groundbreaking game, a graphical adventure inspired by the text-based games that were popular across university campuses in those years.[13] The game was simply named *Adventure* and it allowed players to move in a virtual world that spanned different screens while facing dragons and other challenges in the search for an enchanted chalice to be returned to the king in the golden castle.

Adventure's box. This is the game that started the action/adventure genre, where players could perform real-time actions by using a representation of the player without the need of typing any text. It was also the first game to graphically represent a world bigger than the screen.

---

[13] See the section on *Zork* for more information on this genre, which was a staple of gaming at the time.

Despite the crude graphics (VCS games had to fit in 4 KB only), the possibility of having direct control over the avatar while manipulating objects graphically by using the joystick instead of typing allowed *Adventure* to deliver a unique experience and skyrocketed its sales to more than a million copies.

However, Robinett knew from the very beginning that he would receive no royalties, and that no one would ever know he was the author. This led him to hide a credits page that included his name in a secret room, accessible only by finding a hidden key in the form of a grey pixel stuck on a grey wall. The room wasn't discovered until after Warren had left Atari[14] in 1980, and from that day on it became commonplace to call any hidden surprise found in video games an "easter egg." Robinett's easter egg was a huge and upsetting surprise to Atari. However, something even more revolutionary was on the horizon.

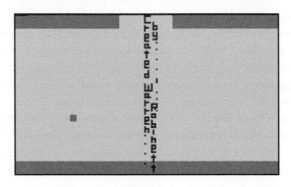

The secret credits room in *Adventure*, the first easter egg in the history of video games.

Everything started when a group of four programmers, Alan Miller, Larry Kaplan, Bob Whitehead, and David Crane, tried to renegotiate the terms of their contract, suggesting guidelines commonly used for musicians and writers. Unfortunately, this new contract was rejected, causing Miller, Whitehead, and Crane to leave Atari. They didn't leave the gaming industry though, and together with an experienced manager from the music industry they started a new company named Activision in October 1979. Kaplan joined them soon afterward and the group started developing new games for the VCS on their own, finding instant success (see the figure on the top of the opposite page).

Inspired by Activision's success, other programmers left Atari, and a second company, Imagic, was formed less than two years later in 1981. Imagic was soon known for its high quality and distinctive productions featuring state-of-the-art graphics and shiny boxes (see the second figure on the opposite page).

---

[14] Robinett continued his successful career by developing educational games and founding The Learning Company as well as working on different virtual reality projects.

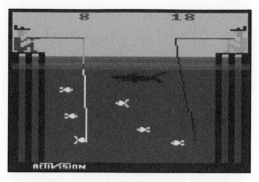

Fishing Derby, one of Activision's four launching titles,[15] released in 1980 for the Atari VCS. This release marked the birth of third-party game development and publishing.

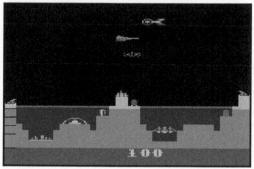

Atlantis, an early Imagic game for the VCS published in 1982. Imagic was one of the most respected developers in the early 1980s.

The management at Atari realized things were getting out of hand. Kassar angrily declared that Activision was "a parasite in the game industry," and unsuccessfully sued the new company several times. His goal was to forbid Activision from developing games for the VCS and from "stealing" a share of their software market, but he was never able to achieve it. Ultimately, Atari had to acknowledge the new developments in the industry and finally changed its internal politics to allow developers to participate in a royalty scheme that turned some of their engineers into millionaires.

Intellivision, ColecoVision, and the Others

Competition for the VCS started in 1978 when Magnavox (which in the meantime became a Philips subsidiary) released the Odyssey[2] (see the figure on page 34). This system was distributed and marketed in Europe directly by Philips under the name

---

[15] The others were *Dragster*, *Boxing*, and *Checkers*.

The Magnavox Odyssey², released in 1978. By 1983, about one million units were sold in the United States and almost an equal number in Europe. The keyboard made it very suitable for educational games, and following the Odyssey's original attempt of supporting traditional board games from the video screen, interesting role playing games (RPGs) in the style of *Dungeons & Dragons* were developed with much success.

Videopac G7000 and it showcased a membrane keyboard for a more serious, computer-like interaction plus a very interesting speech synthesis module. However, its actual success was limited because it didn't manage to create a user base large enough to attract third-party developers. Only Imagic and Parker Brothers developed a few good titles for the system. At this time, after Activision's early successes, it was clear that third-party development was crucial to the survival of any system and this lack of support ultimately left the Odyssey² behind other competitors.

Among the other companies interested in entering the video game industry was Mattel. The toymaker giant soon formed a subsidiary named Mattel Electronics with the sole purpose of developing electronic games. Their first foray in electronic entertainment during the late seventies with simple handheld games was quite successful and they knew the time was right for a bigger involvement. The Mattel Intellivision console was available by 1979 and mass marketed in 1980 at a retail price of $299. It was based on a General Instruments CP1610 microprocessor[16] and was a very innovative product from many perspectives.

---

[16] Some people consider the Intellivision to be the first 16-bit game system because the CP1610 worked with 16-bit registers and addresses. However, CPU instructions were only 10-bit.

The Intellivision console. It had the best graphics when released and, like the whole industry, peaked in 1982, selling more than three million units before the 1983 game market crash.

The Intellivision was the first console to allow 16 different colors on the screen simultaneously plus eight hardware-supported sprites that offered collision detection, mirroring, and stretching. There were also plans to expand the system to reach full computer and multimedia functionalities with a docking station that featured a keyboard and cassette drive as well as several other devices like a voice synthesis module (the "Intellivoice")[17] and a dedicated cable modem, the "PlayCable," for downloading games.[18]

Another element of originality in the Intellivision console was its controllers, which included a numeric keypad plus two buttons on each side and a disk capable of turning the player in 16 different directions (see the figure on the top of page 36).

However, the controller was very difficult to get used to and specific overlays had to be inserted for each game to see what function was dedicated to each key (see the second figure on page 36). This system developed its fans, though, and contributed to turning the Intellivision into the first console for hard-core gamers who were not afraid of a more complex control scheme in exchange for a more rewarding and technologically advanced experience.

---

[17] While devices like the Intellivoice were actually delivered, the promised docking computer keyboard had a lot of issues during prototype stage. Only about 4,000 units were produced for a closed beta testing program but, unfortunately, they were considered unreliable and called back. The project was officially cancelled in 1982, leaving many customers disillusioned and even prompting the Federal Trade Commission to investigate Mattel for false advertising. Mattel was ordered to pay a fine for each month of delay starting in 1982. To avoid paying the fine, Mattel released a much simpler Entertainment Computer System (ECS) add-on to be matched with its redesigned Intellivision II.

[18] In 1981, a subscription-based service was made available to download selected Intellivision games that were continuously broadcast over dedicated cable TV channels, effectively pioneering a new means of distribution that was destined to become very popular in the years to come.

The complex Intellivision controller—a distinctive feature that was copied by other systems that followed soon after but was forgotten by the mid-eighties.

In addition to Mattel's in-house development team, nicknamed the Blue Rangers, all the most important software houses of the time produced games for the system. These included Activision, Imagic, and several others, collectively supplying a good variety of titles that helped the console quickly gain a sizeable share of the market.

On the marketing side, Mattel opted for an aggressive face-to-face campaign against the Atari VCS to promote the better visuals of their system.

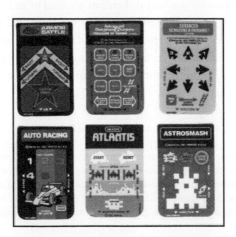

Keypad overlays for some Intellivision games to be put on the controller. A total of 125 games were developed for the system.

A Mattel advertisement comparing baseball games for the VCS and the Intellivision, featuring well-known journalist and writer George Plimpton (1927–2003).

This direct approach fueled the first "console war" among young users that has been common ever since. Atari had the bigger catalogue and range of titles while the Intellivision had better graphics, so both fan groups had strong points when quarrelling. In any case, another serious competitor with even better graphics would emerge at the apex of video game popularity in 1982.

Coleco followed Intellivision by releasing a system that was supposed to be highly expandable through different modules, which, ultimately, would be integrated into a full-fledged computer: the Adam. The console was named ColecoVision and released in August 1982.

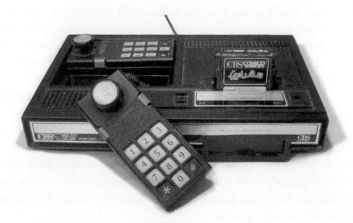

The ColecoVision. A great console built around the Zilog Z-80 processor, which had a very short lifespan due to the imminent industry crash; note the Intellivision-inspired controllers, but with a joystick instead of a disk.

Sega's *Zaxxon* ported to the ColecoVision; it was the closest you could get to the arcade version while staying at home.

The ColecoVision showcased the best graphics seen in any home system up to that day (as many as 32 sprites could be displayed simultaneously) and this made it the best choice for porting arcade games, including those in isometric perspective like *Zaxxon*. It was also the first cross-platform system, featuring an expansion module able to play Atari VCS games. Obviously, Atari didn't like it and sued Coleco, with Coleco countersuing Atari for infringing antitrust laws. In the end, the dispute was settled with Coleco paying a royalty on every expansion module sold.

Well aware of their technical prowess, Coleco executives started hunting for good deals with arcade game developers and they succeeded in obtaining a six-month exclusive license for what was going to become the most popular game of 1982: *Donkey Kong* by Nintendo (see the next section). *Donkey Kong* was then bundled with the console, driving very high sales through the end of 1982 when almost one million units were moved in just a few months, instantly turning Coleco into a major force within the video game industry.

Due to this successful partnership and to ColecoVision's unique capabilities to render Nintendo's arcade games properly, Coleco and Nintendo were quite closely tied at a certain point. So close, in fact, that Nintendo proposed to Coleco an agreement to distribute and sell ColecoVision in Japan. The two companies, though, couldn't reach an agreement on the economic terms[19] and negotiations were abandoned when Nintendo declared it would design its own system instead.

Overall, the ColecoVision made a huge impression but the fast-changing conditions in the industry prevented it from fully realizing its potential. About 125 games were produced and around two million units were sold before the console was officially discontinued in 1985.

Among the plethora of video game systems released in those early years with little or no success, one is especially worth remembering: the Vectrex. The Vectrex was first showcased at the Summer Consumer Electronics Show (CES) in Chicago in 1982 and went on sale in time for Christmas at $199.

---

[19] Nintendo wanted to buy the console at 10% above production costs while Coleco wanted to sell it at a 10% discount from retail price.

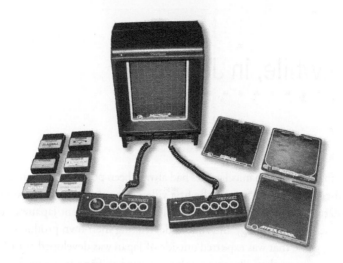

The Vectrex with a few game cartridges and screen overlays. These were used to provide a colorful backdrop since the vector graphics were in black and white only.

Designed by Jay Smith for General Consumer Electronics, it was the first home console based on vector technology with a built-in nine-inch monitor. Its design made it perfect to play arcade-style games like *Asteroids* or *Tempest* and the system received great praise from the specialized press. The lack of color probably didn't appeal to more casual players, though, who saw the use of screen overlays as too cumbersome and old-fashioned. Despite this, the Vectrex was a truly original console that even showcased some very special add-ons, like a set of glasses named 3D Imager, which, by quickly opening and closing each eye's window in sync with the console to properly alternate the images for the left and right eye, could simulate a 3D experience. Only 30 games were developed and the console was soon discontinued in 1984.

An original ad for the Vectrex, including the 3D Imager and a light pen.

Meanwhile, in Japan…

• • • • • • • • • • • • • •

Arcades with electro-mechanical games had always been popular in Japan. It shouldn't be a surprise, then, that as soon as the first video games from Atari and other manufacturers started arriving in the Land of the Rising Sun, different Japanese companies embraced the new technology and started developing their own products.

The first game that was exported outside of Japan was developed as early as 1975 by Taito, a company that, like many others, started shifting its focus from vending and pinball machines to the new genre of entertainment. The game was originally called *Western Gun* and, due to its Wild West theme featuring a two-cowboy shootout, it was considered a good export candidate. Midway agreed to import it in North America and renamed it *Gun Fight*. Nutting Associates was also involved in modifying the game by including an Intel 8080 processor for a smoother handling of the graphics, thus turning it into the first arcade game to leave Japan and the first one to use a CPU.

Flyer from Midway presenting *Gun Fight*, developed by Taito in 1975 and then perfected by Nutting. It was the first Japanese game to be imported in the United States (by Midway) and to use a CPU.

Though *Gun Fight* wasn't a memorable game, customers didn't have to wait long before the first gaming sensation from Japan hit the worldwide scene. In 1978, Taito released another game based on the 8080 processor and designed by Tomohiro Nishikado (born 1944). It was named *Space Invaders* and put the player in charge of defending a planet from hordes of slowly descending aliens. The immediateness of the concept, plus the escalating tension and excitement due to the inexorable advancement of the aliens, made this an instant hit and popularized video games even further.

In Japan, the game was so successful that *Space Invaders* machines started popping up everywhere, including grocery stores. Everyone played it all over the country whenever possible, even provoking a shortage of 100 ¥ coins across Japan. The game was soon distributed worldwide and had similar success everywhere,[20] starting the shoot-'em-up genre and inspiring countless different games, clones, and remakes to this day.

Space Invaders was so successful that Atari realized its importance as a strategic title and acquired the rights for porting it to its own VCS console. After *Pong*, this was another game entering homes from the arcades and it was obviously an excellent choice—the official conversion released in 1980 was a system-seller that helped skyrocket VCS sales.

Japanese evergreen classics were not going to stop, though, and different companies started releasing great new games on a regular basis. In 1980, it was Namco's turn

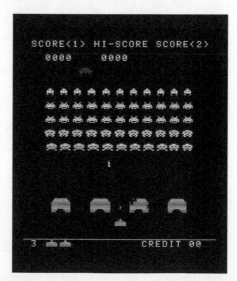

The original *Space Invaders*. Graphics were in black and white, and color was simulated in some cabinets by simply using a colored glass on top of the display (green for the player's ship and bunkers, red for the flying saucer in the upper part of the screen).

---

[20] It is estimated that the game earned Taito about $500 million.

to create not only a successful game but the most iconic game character of all time, thanks to the imagination of game designer Toru Iwatani (born 1955): Puck-Man.

At a time when most games were based on shooting, Pac-Man brought the maze-chase genre to new heights. The cute, colorful graphics, together with the game's attention to detail and short cut scenes, which are noninteractive animation sequences usually used to advance the plot in the game and introduce all the characters involved (each with its unique features and names), were able to attract players regardless of gender, turning it into a worldwide social phenomenon. Pac-Man soon spawned the first video game-related brand, with merchandise of all types featuring the game characters being sold. Even a song, *Pac-Man Fever*, was successfully released and climbed up to the #9 spot in the American charts. Not surprisingly, *Pac-Man* was also the first game to inspire a guide-book[21] along with its exciting competitive play for many years to come.[22]

Another unforgettable game was released just one year later by a company that was relatively unknown outside of Japan: Nintendo. The game was *Donkey Kong* and it was designed by Shigeru Miyamoto (born 1952).

Original flyer for Puck-Man (1980). The character was soon renamed Pac-Man when exported in the United States for fear that inappropriate vandalism was too tempting.

---

[21] Ken Uston, *Mastering Pac Man*. New York: Signet, 1981.

[22] On July 4, 1999, Billy Mitchell scored, for the first time ever, a perfect game worth 3,333,360 points.

A screenshot from the American version of *Pac-Man* introducing the four ghosts who relentlessly chase the player through the maze.

Donkey Kong was a special game in many respects. Not only was it the first "platform" game featuring a jumping mechanic and thus starting a completely new genre, but it was also the first game to tell a simple yet entertaining story by means of short cut scenes. These worked perfectly to immerse players into the game and make them follow the events of a stubborn gorilla escaping and then kidnapping the girlfriend of its owner—a cute, short man with red and blue dress known as "Jumpman the carpenter." Jumpman was eventually renamed Mario, changed into an Italian plumber, and became a video game icon as famous as Pac-Man.

Shigeru Miyamoto, arguably the most successful and influential game designer ever.

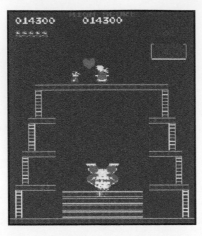

The final screen: at last Donkey Kong is defeated. Jumpman and his lady can be happy together... but not for long, as the action starts all over again at a higher level of difficulty.

Donkey Kong was split across four different levels that Jumpman had to go through to reach his beloved while avoiding several obstacles. At the end, he would finally defeat the gorilla and save the girl. Interestingly, *Donkey Kong* was also at the center of an amusing legal case. Both Nintendo and Coleco (who had just licensed the game for its ColecoVision system) were sued by Universal City Studios since they thought the game infringed on their King Kong copyrights. While Coleco was keen on settling the matter as soon as possible and started paying a 3% royalty to Universal, Nintendo decided to fight in court where they easily won. They demonstrated that Universal itself proved, in a previous legal case in 1975 against RKO Pictures (the original makers of the *King Kong* movie in 1933), that the iconic gorilla was considered part of the public domain.

This impressive string of successes catapulted Japanese games to the worldwide stage and made their respective companies hugely popular. Furthermore, the field of arcade games was not the only one in which Japanese ingenuity would shine, and different groups started trying their hands at consoles too. After a first attempt in 1981 by Epoch with an extremely rare console named Cassette Vision, things started getting more exciting by July 1983 when two systems were released simultaneously by Sega and Nintendo.

Sega was founded in 1940 in Hawaii as Standard Games to provide coin-operated amusement machines such as jukeboxes. It moved to Japan in 1952 under the name Service Games of Japan and was later renamed Sega Enterprises. The company started working on electro-mechanical games in the mid-sixties and then moved to video games in the seventies. In 1983, they were ready to enter the home market with the SG-1000, their first consumer electronics product and the starting point for several successful consoles to follow.

The Sega SG-1000, built around an NEC 780C (a Z-80 clone), was able to handle a screen resolution of 256 × 192 pixels plus 32 sprites and 16 different colors at once.

The SG-1000, though, encountered only moderate success. It faced both internal competition from the SC-3000 (a simple home computer released in the same year that was architecturally identical to it and able to play all its games, in addition to allowing users to write their own programs in BASIC) and, more importantly, from the other new console on the market: the Famicom.

Nintendo's console, meaning "family computer," was designed by Masayuki Uemura (born 1943) and turned out to be a fantastic machine. It was built on a modified version of the MOS 6502 CPU (specifically, a Ricoh 2A03), incorporating custom sound hardware and an innovative Ricoh picture processing unit (PPU) to offer a more effective way of handling sounds and graphics compared to other systems. After a false start due to a defective chip that forced Nintendo to recall all consoles and change the motherboard, sales increased instantly and half a million units were sold by the end of the year.

The original Nintendo Famicom as released in 1983 in Japan. Launch titles included beloved classics like Nintendo's own *Donkey Kong* and *Popeye*.

Nintendo executives were very confident of their upcoming success and wanted to release it in the United States as soon as possible. Nintendo contacted Atari in early 1983 and offered a licensing agreement in which the American company would acquire the rights to manufacture Nintendo's console and market it under its own brand name.

Kassar was very interested in getting his hands on the Famicom. Atari was secretly designing a new console, the 7800, and Ray wisely thought that if the Famicom turned out to be the better system, Atari would still earn money by licensing and selling it, while if the 7800 was the winner, they wouldn't have risked much anyway. Most likely, though, trying to enter the American scene at that time would have probably resulted in a serious strategic error—the whole industry was in a deep crisis and people were losing confidence and interest in video games (see Part II). It would have been much better to wait until the storm was over and, luckily, this is exactly what happened due to the big corporate changes affecting Atari; Kassar was removed from his CEO position before the negotiations could end and nothing was ultimately done.

Nintendo had to wait until 1985 before having a chance to distribute the Famicom overseas, under the name Nintendo Entertainment System, but this is a different story that will be told later in the book.

Computers Go Home Too!

• • • • • • • • • • • • • • • • • •

Arcades and home consoles were not the only possible ways people could experience video games. Among the first to realize the appeal of a "personal computer" were Steve Jobs and Steve Wozniak who, after short stints at Atari and HP, respectively, started Apple Computer.[23] Apple's first product, the Apple I, was showcased at the Homebrew Computer Club in Palo Alto, California, in July 1976 and sold for $666.66 (about $2,500 adjusted for inflation as of 2009). It was just an assembled circuit board that hobbyists used to build their own system by adding casing, a power supply, a keyboard, and a monitor.

More complete models were already in the works, though, spurring even more interest in this new branch of the electronic industry. Commodore soon showcased the PET, Apple presented the first iteration of the Apple II, and Tandy RadioShack announced the TRS-80 (see the figures on page 48). All models had similar capabilities (all mounted only 4KB of RAM in their basic configuration since memory was very expensive at the time) but each had its unique strengths: the Apple was the only one capable of displaying up to six colors simultaneously, the PET had a built-in monitor and could display both uppercase and lowercase letters, and the TRS-80 could rely on RadioShack's impressive distribution chain. All computers were released within a few months in 1977 and, henceforth, were granted the "1977 Trinity" nickname by Byte magazine. Atari and Texas Instruments soon joined the group by releasing different models in 1979. Atari produced the 400 and 800 models, while TI introduced the TI99/4 (see the figures on page 49).

Even though simple games started appearing very early for all these machines, gaming was not their natural focus—these first personal computers were quite expensive, usually retailing at a price close to $1,000 or even higher, so their appeal was primarily confined to professional users or wealthy and technology-oriented hobbyists. To bring the industry to a new level of awareness and to penetrate deeper into society by also capturing the average person, a new approach to the market was needed.

---

[23] Apple was incorporated on April 1, 1976. See the game *Breakout* in the Games That Pushed Boundaries I section to find out more about Steve Jobs' beginnings at Atari.

The original Apple II released in 1977. Built with a MOS 6502 at its core, it was sold for $1,298. It was the only computer released in 1977 featuring a color display.

The Tandy/RadioShack TRS-80 Model I, which retailed for $599. Its CPU was a Zilog Z-80.

The Commodore PET 2001. It used a MOS 6502 and sold for $795. It was the first computer entirely designed and produced by Commodore.

The Atari 400 (left) and 800 (right) computers released in 1979 for $549.95 and $999.95, respectively. The 400 was considered an introductory computer for gamers while the 800 targeted a more "professional" audience in direct competition with the Apple II. The two computers were almost identical, though, with the latter having 8 KB RAM instead of 4 KB and a better, more professional keyboard. Both were using a MOS 6502 processor.

The TI99/4, released in 1979 by Texas Instruments, was sold for $1,195 including a color monitor. It used TI's own TMS 9900 CPU.

Jack Tramiel and Commodore

Jack Tramiel (born 1928) was one of the most iconic figures in the computer industry in the seventies and eighties and almost singlehandedly succeeded in defining the new concept of the "home computer."

Of Polish and Jewish descent (he was born Idek Trzmiel), Jack was captured by the Nazis at the beginning of World War II and sent to the infamous concentration

Jack Tramiel, founder of Commodore and the person who successfully brought computers into the homes of millions of people.

camp at Auschwitz. Aware that workers had to be fed, he survived for years by volunteering to build roads while people around him were killed. When the war was finally over and he regained his freedom, he fled to the United States.

To pay his debt to a country that became his new home, Jack served for a short while in the US Army where he learned to repair typewriters and other office equipment. In 1953, while working as a taxi driver in New York, he started a small typewriter repair shop in the Bronx, marking the beginning of Commodore. The company was then relocated to Toronto where Jack moved in 1955, hoping to find more opportunities and less competition. From office furniture and typewriters, Commodore soon moved to manufacturing calculators and conquered a sizeable share of the market until Texas Instruments, thanks to its own "vertical integration"[24] strategy, started a price war by lowering prices to points that were not sustainable for other companies. Many were driven out of business and Commodore barely survived. This defeat taught Jack a very important lesson, which he would soon put into practice.

The first step towards Commodore's renaissance was to ask Irving Gould (c. 1915–2004), a well-known Canadian investor and Commodore's main shareholder, to approve and finance the acquisition of MOS Technology in 1976. MOS was a semiconductor company that had just developed a new 8-bit microprocessor, the 6502. This strategic acquisition gave Commodore the opportunity to pioneer the personal computer market, together with Apple and Tandy, but with a fundamental difference: they were now able to use in-house technology. In fact, having

---

[24] This is a business approach where the same company owns all the different aspects of making, selling, and delivering a product or service.

MOS as one of its own subsidiaries allowed Commodore to implement effectively a vertical integration approach that became the main keyword in Jack's aggressive business style.

Jack's unique approach was nicknamed The Religion, and practicing it was a fundamental principle that every Commodore executive had to bear in mind, starting with one of Jack's most famous quotes, "Business is war." Some important aspects of The Religion that made Commodore unique were:

- Don't hire people who need to learn the job; you hire people to do the job, not to learn about it.

- Fire people fast. At Commodore, managers who were fired often had to leave on the spot—they could go back to clear out their office a couple of days later.

- Don't try to negotiate a deal unless you can walk away.[25]

- Everyone has to be involved (i.e., managers have to do the job, not just manage others who do the job for them).

In addition to these personal rules, Tramiel had another attitude that made him completely different from more traditional business people like Ray Kassar. Kassar used to focus all his energies and attention on a bestselling item, even at the risk of harming his own company's new products and ideas (like what happened with the VCS and Cosmos). Tramiel, on the other hand, believed that to remain ahead of the competition, one had to constantly compete with oneself and keep innovating.

In late 1979, the first batch of personal computers from Apple, Tandy, Atari, and Commodore were raising more and more interest, but they still remained too expensive for the average person to buy. At this point, Jack decided they had to "sell to the masses, not to the classes" and, during a general meeting in early 1980, he interrupted the other managers by shouting, "Gentlemen, the Japanese are coming, so we will become the Japanese!"

Fearing that the Japanese were soon going to launch some new low-cost computer, Commodore had to arrive first and conquer the new market. This is where the idea of a low-cost color computer originated and the project started taking shape in the following months under the supervision of Michael Tomczyk. Tomcyzk's idea was to market this new machine, named VIC-20, as the first "friendly computer," something that was completely unheard of before.

---

[25] This rule made Jack Tramiel one of the toughest negotiators in the business. For example, when discussing with a young Bill Gates about licensing Microsoft BASIC for all Commodore machines in the late seventies, Bill wanted a $3 royalty on every computer sold. In the end, Jack signed for a onetime payment of only $25,000, telling Bill that he was "already married" and was not going to accept any long-term commitment. Considering the millions of machines that Commodore was going to sell in the coming years, this was an amazing deal.

The VIC-20, released first in Japan as the VIC-1001 in late 1980 and then worldwide starting from January 1981, was the first color computer to target the masses by retailing at only $299.95—about half the price of any other machine with similar features available at the time. The VIC had 5 KB of RAM (expandable), several peripherals, and a joystick port for games. More than 250 games were developed for it, both from Commodore and from third-party developers.

Because they were low-cost and very popular, video games seemed like a very suitable application and became one of the main features that Commodore decided to emphasize for marketing the VIC, putting it into direct competition with the gaming console of the time. Concurrently, a dedicated in-house team developed several titles, usually inspired by well-known arcade games. Published titles included *Vic-Avengers*, a clone of *Space Invaders*, plus a few games licensed from Namco like *Radar Rat Race* (see the figure on the opposite page), a variation of the arcade game *Rally-X*, and *Jelly Monsters*, a very nice *Pac-Man* clone that angered Atari who had previously bought the exclusive rights for home consoles and was working on its own version.

"Why buy just a video game?" An ad page featuring actor William Shatner (Captain Kirk in the famous *Star Trek* TV series) comparing the VIC-20 to gaming consoles like the Atari and Intellivision, and showing how it could offer much more at a comparable price.

Box art for the game *Radar Rat Race*, one of the VIC launch titles internally developed by Commodore engineers.

The VIC-20 was a huge success that went beyond even Commodore's own expectations. It was the first computer ever to sell more than one million units,[26] catapulting Commodore into the arena of home entertainment while paving the way for all other "home" machines to come, including the bestselling Commodore 64.

Across the Pond: Sinclair

Commodore was not the only company to work on inexpensive computers. Sinclair Instrument (later renamed Sinclair Research) was a British company incorporated in 1973 in Cambridge by Sir Clive Sinclair (born 1940) who had previous experience in radio and high fidelity (hi-fi) R&D due to an earlier business named Sinclair Radionics in the sixties. The new company started developing innovative electronic devices in the mid-seventies, first with digital watches and pocket TVs and later with home computers and several other futuristic projects in the following years.

Even before Jack Tramiel, Sinclair thought the first personal computers were overpriced and out of reach for most people, so he pushed forward to design a simple machine that was affordable for anyone. The first computer to be officially released was the ZX-80 in 1980. It was a basic machine with 1 KB RAM and 4 KB ROM (which included a BASIC interpreter, editor, and a simple OS) that was sold as a kit through postal orders for less than £100 or already assembled at a slightly higher price.

---

[26] Overall, the VIC-20 sold more than two million units worldwide.

The Sinclair ZX-80. It mounted a Zilog Z-80 equivalent processor manufactured by NEC.

To keep manufacturing costs down, Sinclair relied on software instead of hardware for most of the ZX-80 tasks, including generating the video signal. This had serious consequences though; for example, when pressing a key, the system had to switch off the video signal quickly to be able to process the input before showing it again on the screen, producing a very tedious flickering effect. Despite its shortcomings, the ZX-80 was relatively successful as it sold about 50,000 units (still a remarkable achievement at the time), and it was soon followed in 1981 by an improved version named ZX-81.

The ZX-81, an improved version of the ZX-80 sold preassembled or as a kit at £69.95 and £49.95, respectively. In addition to a cassette recorder to store programs, a printer was also available, turning this into a complete system that went on to sell 1.5 million units.

3D Monster Maze, released in 1982, showed what talented programmers could achieve even on a rudimentary machine once they mastered all the nuances of the hardware. The game needed the 16 KB RAM expansion and many players were reported to have hit the keys so hard due to their excitement in the attempt to escape the monster that the keyboard often broke or the expansion module disconnected from the system, prompting an instant machine reset.

Like its predecessor, the ZX-81 shipped with only 1 KB RAM, but an expansion module with 16 KB as well as a membrane keyboard was readily available. Although it was unable to provide a color image or any sound, the system's flickering problem was solved and the computer was powerful enough to run simple games including the porting of several successful titles and the running of its original ones. Among these, the most popular game was *3D Monster Maze* by Malcolm Evans, a game that managed to show a first-person 3D perspective to immerse players in a hectic maze chase where they had to escape from a hungry *Tyrannosaurus rex*.

Sinclair's computers were quite popular across Europe throughout the eighties but they didn't meet with any meaningful success in North America where they were distributed by Timex,[27] or in other markets.

---

[27] For example, the ZX-81 was marketed in the United States as the Timex-Sinclair 1000 at a price of $100. People at Commodore used them as doorstoppers.

Games That Pushed Boundaries I

In this section, as well as in related sections to follow, we will review some very influential games that were not discussed previously. These games had an everlasting influence by affecting specific game genres, or even the industry as a whole, by implementing new concepts and ideas. Let us begin by looking at games, whether from arcades, consoles, or home computers, that were developed before the video game crash of 1983.

Breakout (1976, Atari)

Breakout, where players had to use a paddle to bounce a ball and destroy a series of blocks, was designed by a young Atari employee named Steve Jobs based upon an original idea from Nolan Bushnell. The game was implemented by one of Jobs' friends, Steve Wozniak, who, despite being a Hewlett-Packard employee, still found enough time to work on this project. (According to his own memories, he didn't sleep for three days straight in order to complete the design.)

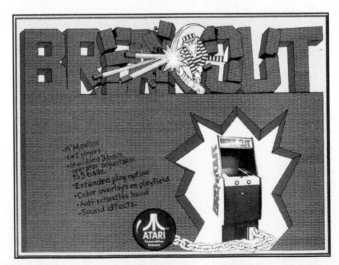

Original *Breakout* arcade flyer.

The game was outstanding not only because it provided a new life to the ball-and-paddle genre that seemed definitely over after the *Pong* craze, but also because of Wozniak's amazing minimalist design that featured a circuit board with only 20+ chips (the average game had around 75). Unfortunately, the new design was so difficult to understand that before moving into actual production, Atari engineers decided to redo it from scratch by using as many as 100 integrated circuits because they couldn't figure out how it actually worked. It was common practice to give a bonus of $100 or more for every chip removed from the average target of 75 as an incentive to reduce manufacturing costs, and Jobs was awarded a several-thousand-dollar bonus.[28]

The new game turned out to be a huge success, selling tens of thousands of cabinets worldwide. It was so successful, in fact, that not only were many games spawned by it (including excellent titles like *Arkanoid* by Taito in 1986), but even whole game cabinets were counterfeited and sold to arcades as Atari machines. In Japan, for example, the game's success even attracted the attention of the Yakuza (the local organized crime syndicates) who started manufacturing and selling pirated copies of the games themselves.

In the end, *Breakout's* influence was deeper than one typically expects from a single, even very successful game and it turned out to affect the development of the whole computer industry. In fact, according to Wozniak, the game actually determined his design for the Apple II: "A lot of features of the Apple II went in because I had designed *Breakout* for Atari. I had designed it in hardware. I wanted to write it in software now."[29] So he started adding sound and graphical capabilities to the new computer in order to facilitate the subsequent coding of games like *Breakout*.

Night Driver (1977, Atari)

Though not the first racing game (*Grand Track 10*, as seen previously, arrived first), *Night Driver* changed the user experience by allowing for a new degree of immersion despite the very limited computational means available.

For the first time, a game took place from the player's own perspective and the track was seen moving under the player's eyes in a first-person view. Since the technology of the time didn't allow for suitable graphics, the night setting was actually a simple excuse to have a completely black background while the track was identified by road-side reflectors. The car shape was just a rectangle that was usually enhanced by adding a plastic layer to represent a more realistic silhouette on the video cabinet

---

[28] Jobs didn't share the bonus with Wozniak, who found out about it only a few years later and obviously wasn't too happy.

[29] Connick, Jack. "...And Then There Was Apple". *Call-A.P.P.L.E.* Oct 1986: 24.

Night Driver. For the first time, players got to sit in the driver's seat.

in the arcade. Despite all of these shortcomings, though, the design was effective and for the first time players had a real illusion of speed while driving in a video game.

Asteroids (1979, Atari)

Designed and programmed by Ed Logg, *Asteroids* was another of Atari's big arcade successes. The game was set in space where the player had to destroy as many asteroids and hostile saucers as possible without being hit. A unique feature was that when big asteroids were hit, they split into smaller and faster ones, making the action increasingly hectic.

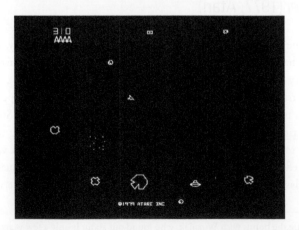

Asteroids was Atari's second title, after *Lunar Lander*, to use a new vector technology developed in house (the Digital Vector Generator [DVG]) that allowed crisper and higher resolution graphics.

Despite a difficult set of controls (no joystick, but different buttons to rotate the ship, shoot, thrust, and hyper-jump), the game was able to attract countless players thanks to its sharp vector graphics, simple but effective sound (often compared to a "heart beat," which increased its pace as more asteroids were destroyed), and, most importantly, a leader board that allowed players to write their initials or three-letter nicknames. This offered new possibilities for competitions between players who could now prove who was the best player in the arcade. In a matter of months, all games started having a leader board and soon the first gaming competitions were organized and high scores officially recorded.[30] Due to *Asteroid's* lasting popularity, sequels and ports to most home consoles and computers were also developed in the following years.

Galaxian (1979, Namco)

At a time when many games still relied on plastic overlays to provide color, *Galaxian* brought graphics appeal to a new level by showing multicolored animated sprites, explosions, colored fonts for writing the high score, and a moving star field in the background.

Galaxian promotional flyer. Multicolored sprites brought a new level of fun to the alien-shooting action.

---

[30] While playing *Asteroids* on November 13, 1982, Scott Safran from Cherry Hill, New Jersey, set the unbeaten world record of 41,336,440 points by playing for more than 20 hours non-stop.

The gameplay was also innovative; though clearly inspired by *Space Invaders*, it pushed the envelope further by allowing more complex alien movements that were not easily predictable. The attacking waves, for example, could swarm all around the screen trying to hit the player, adding more excitement to the action.

Galaxian was successfully ported to all major computers of the early eighties (like the Commodore VIC-20 and 64, ZX Spectrum, Apple II, and Atari 400/800 and MSX), plus Atari 2600 and 5200 consoles.

Star Raiders (1979, Atari)

Released for the Atari 400 and 800 computers and designed by Doug Neubauer, *Star Raiders* soon developed a cult following thanks to its immersive qualities that had many people losing sleep in order to play.

What made this game so unique and addicting? First, it successfully combined sci-fi elements that were very popular at the time. References to movies and TV series like *Star Wars* and *Star Trek* were clearly evident, with players dividing their time between action/combat sequences in open space and more strategic/planning sessions spent studying a galactic map to decide on the next destination. The technical implementation was also extremely well done, with the player put right into the spaceship's control seat thanks to a moving star field originating from a single focal point, thus providing an effective first-person feeling.

Star Raiders' box—by far the most successful title on the first generation of Atari 8-bit computers.

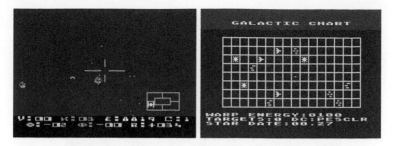

In the middle of combat (left) and planning the next move on the galactic map (right).

Despite its complex controls and the fact that it required a proper computer keyboard to navigate the spaceships, *Star Raiders* was such a hit that Atari ported it in 1982 to its own consoles.[31] Its influence was long lasting, even affecting franchises developed many years later like *Wing Commander* (1990, Origin Systems) and the *Star Wars: X-Wing* series (1993, LucasArts).

Zork (1979, Infocom)

College students' thirst for games wasn't quenched by *Spacewar!* and small groups of enthusiasts kept experimenting with new concepts in many universities throughout the sixties and seventies. Most mainframes of the time, though, had very limited output capabilities—often consisting of only text output from a printer—making text-based games the only available choice.

Among these, two projects had a special influence on the history of games: *Dungeon* by Don Daglow in 1975, the first adventure/RPG based on the recent *Dungeons & Dragons* board game, and *Colossal Cave Adventure* by William Crowther and Don Woods (developed on a PDP-10 between 1975 and 1977). These pioneering games, besides influencing different people like Ken and Roberta Williams, founders of On-Line Software,[32] or Roy Trubshaw and Richard Bartle who developed *MUD* (*Multi-User Dungeon*, the first online multiplayer game) between 1978 and 1980, also inspired a group of MIT students in 1977 to start a new project. This project was named *Zork* and became a landmark in the rising interactive fiction genre.

Zork was set in a vast underground labyrinth where the player, a nameless adventurer, was free to roam in search of treasures while facing different creatures and dangers. It was an especially rich and fascinating game thanks not only to its engaging

---

[31] With a 38-page manual, it was considered the most complex and fascinating game ever released on the otherwise ill-fated Atari 5200 console.

[32] Later renamed Sierra Entertainment.

Zork I : The Great Underground Empire original box art.

and often humorous storytelling but also for the quality of its text parser that allowed a complex and natural interaction with the user. It accepted input phrases not limited to a verb-noun syntax like earlier games, but also including prepositions and conjunctions (e.g., "kill the goblin with the elvish sword").

The game received such high interest and enthusiastic feedback that some of its original programmers decided to start a company named Infocom in 1979 to release the game commercially into a trilogy: *Zork I: The Great Underground Empire* released in 1980, *Zork II: The Wizard of Frobozz* released in 1981, and *Zork III: The Dungeon Master* released in 1982. The trilogy attained instant success on every computer to which it was ported.

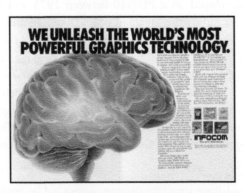

An ad by Infocom to support the immersive qualities of text-based games in a market that was getting increasingly graphics-oriented.

With *Zork*, Infocom popularized the nascent text adventure genre that was extremely popular throughout the mid-eighties and faded only when computers' graphical capabilities became so rich that they were considered a required addition to properly enhance the players' experience. After being acquired by Activision in 1986, at a time when text-only games were already past their prime, Infocom was ultimately closed in 1989.

Tail Gunner (1979, Cinematronics)

Larry Rosenthal, an MIT graduate who worked on *SpaceWar!* and who developed an innovative vector-based technology to display sharp images,[33] joined a California-based company named Cinematronics soon after its incorporation in 1975.

Though Cinematronics' first games were neither particularly impressive nor successful, Rosenthal's new technology set the stage for the development of *Tail Gunner*,[34] the first game featuring true 3D vector-based objects. Players were put in command of a gunning station on a large spaceship and enemy fighters could maneuver around nimbly, approaching or moving away from the player, with a realistic effect.

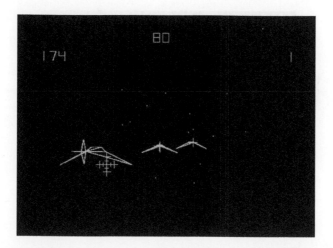

Tail Gunner, released in 1979, was the first true 3D game, using vector graphics to draw lines and animate shapes made by a few polygons.

---

[33] In vector-based monitors, images are drawn by tracing lines from point to point instead of processing all available rows one by one in sequence as in the raster-scan technology typical of all TV sets of the time.

[34] Actually, Rosenthal left Cinematronics to start his own company, Vectorbeam, which, after releasing *Tail Gunner*, was acquired by Cinematronics with all of its assets and intellectual properties.

Defender (1980, Williams)

Designed by Eugene Jarvis for Williams Electronics in 1980, *Defender* was a unique game for many reasons. Not only was it the first 2D side-scrolling shooting game where the player had to fight aliens over a map several times the width of the screen, but, besides fighting, the player also had the duty of protecting hapless humanoid figures from being abducted. These goals perfectly complemented each other, allowing for very fast and exciting action where players could strategize their game in different ways. Thanks to the notable addition of a radar/minimap on the top part of the screen, players could see their own as well as the enemies' positions across the game world.

Though the control scheme was quite complex, featuring a two-way joystick and five buttons that gave *Defender* the reputation as one of the hardest games ever, it also added another challenge for players to master and ultimately contributed to its everlasting appeal, thanks to the never-before-seen colorful explosions and particle effects programmed by Sam Dicker.

About 55,000 *Defender* cabinets were sold and the game grossed about $1 billion during its lifetime, making it Williams's biggest success.

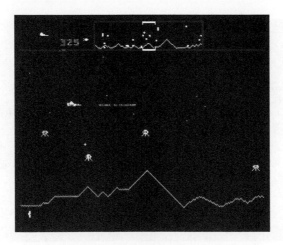

Challenging controls, fighting aliens, and saving people while surfing across a wide landscape amidst colorful explosions—the recipe for *Defender*'s lasting success.

Flight Simulator (1980, SubLogic)

Bruce Artwick started working on his *Flight Simulator* program in 1978 and it was commercially released in January 1980 on the Apple II and Tandy TRS-80. The

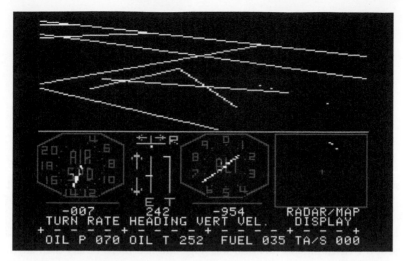

The original *Flight Simulator*. The cockpit view was updated only about 3 to 5 times per second.

game was very simple—there was only one aircraft, equipped with the most basic controls, and one small flying region featuring some mountains and a few buildings. Despite these limitations and its extreme simplicity, the game was able to combine both civilian and military flight actions. In fact, by pressing "W" the pilot could enter the World War I British Ace game mode where he or she had to shoot down enemy planes and bomb their base.

In 1982, SubLogic released *Flight Simulator II*, which was soon licensed by Microsoft to start its well-known franchise.

Ultima (1981, California Pacific Computer Company)

Designed by Richard Garriott and published first by California Pacific Computer Company on the Apple II and then re-released by Origin as *Ultima I: the First Age of Darkness* on different systems including the Commodore 64 and Atari 8-bit home computers, *Ultima* was the game that defined modern RPGs.

The story was pretty original and exciting in 1980 and its theme was to be re-used countless times in the future—the realm of Sosaria had fallen into a time of darkness and despair due to an evil wizard named Mondain. The player was summoned by the righteous king of the land, Lord British, to defeat the evil by finding and destroying the Gem of Power, which was owned by the wizard. The main character was defined by six different attributes (Strength, Stamina, Agility, Charisma, Wisdom, and Intelligence) that could improve during the game, making him increasingly powerful.

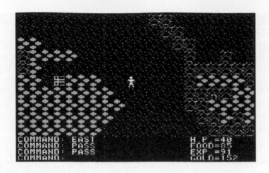

A screenshot from the original *Ultima*. In 1981, the game sold about 30,000 copies on the Apple II.

Ultima was also notable as the first commercial game to use tile graphics to represent the environment. Its world was huge and had more variety than anything seen before: open spaces with forests, lakes, castles, dungeons, etc. were all waiting to be explored and conquered. These features generated for the game an audience big enough to spawn a long-lasting franchise.

Pitfall! (1982, Activision)

Originally published for the Atari VCS and later ported to several other systems including the Sega SG-1000 and home computers like the Commodore 64, *Pitfall!* is regarded by many as the best game ever produced for the VCS. Its author, David Crane (one of the original Activision founders), succeeded in writing a masterpiece of software engineering by developing such a complex and visually appealing game despite the constraints of a standard VCS cartridge (i.e., the whole program had to fit

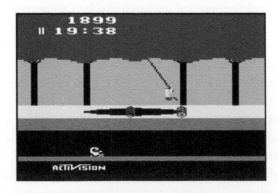

The original *Pitfall!* on the Atari VCS.

in only 4 KB of memory) and showed new possibilities for a console that, though at its peak, was also showing its age.

The game's technical prowess perfectly supported all the references that made the game feel instantly familiar and immersive. Elements from evergreen stories like *Tarzan* or popular cartoons and movies like *Heckle and Jekyll* and the Indiana Jones movie *Raiders of the Lost Ark* were easily recognizable. These features made role-playing as the young explorer, Pitfall Harry, in his quest to recover 32 priceless treasures from a dangerous and unknown jungle split into 254 screens an exciting experience that advanced the action/adventure genre to new heights.

Utopia (1982, Mattel)

An exclusive to the Intellivision console designed by Don Daglow, *Utopia* marked the birth of simulation games with a political flavor, and it can also be regarded as a precursor to real-time strategy (RTS) games.

Utopia for the Intellivision. Sims and RTS games started here.

A two-player game in which each player took control of one island, *Utopia* let people decide how to handle resources and construct different buildings, each with different properties and the ability to affect the environment in a different way. As each island's population grew, players had to be sure enough food was available. Otherwise, rebel activity would arise around the island, decreasing the player's score and eventually destroying the buildings. Players could also try to harm each other by sending rebels to the opposite island. The game would ultimately end after a predefined time to see who was able to obtain the highest score.

Part II

The crash, home computers, and an extra life

1983: The Crash

• • • • • • • • • • •

1982 was a terrific year for the burgeoning video game industry. New systems and software houses were popping up everywhere and hardware sales were phenomenally high for all the main players, including Atari, Intellivision, and the newly-arrived ColecoVision. Unfortunately, this very fast and explosive expansion was carrying also the seeds of its sudden demise and the industry's success would change within a matter of months.

Throughout 1982, Atari executives were confident they would be able to meet a 50% year-over-year increase in sales, as stated in their financial outlooks. However, during the quarterly conference call on December 7, 1982, it was finally declared that the actual growth was only around 10%. The huge miss from the original, overly optimistic estimates sent analysts and investors into a panic. On Wall Street, Warner immediately lost 32% of its market price, falling from $51.75 to $35.13 a share.

While results from other manufacturers like Coleco were still in line with original expectations, suddenly people at all levels—from analysts to executives to developers to gamers—realized there was something wrong throughout the whole industry. This abrupt awakening and consequent pessimism triggered a snowball effect in which people started to lose interest in playing, and more importantly in buying, new games.

How could all of this have happened? There were different reasons that combined to cause the dramatic implosion of the market that was witnessed between 1983 and 1984. Most likely, the main factors involved were:

◘ public perception,

◘ over-saturation and low-quality games,

◘ transitioning to a new generation, and

◘ home computer wars.

We will proceed in analyzing each of these individually to gain a better understanding of what was happening across the industry, and in American society, at that time. After that, we will see how individual companies were affected.

Public Perception

Unfortunately, video games were seen with diffidence and scrutinized under a suspicious light by the general press and public alike since their very early days. In 1976, in fact, *Death Race*, an arcade game somewhat inspired by the cult sci-fi movie *Death Race 2000* (1975), was released and many people began perceiving video games as something "evil," able to excite our worst instincts and negatively impact young people.

Death Race, an arcade game released in 1976 by Exidy where players had to compete by driving a car to run over stylized zombies. Most people, though, felt the objective of the game was to mercilessly run over pedestrians, like in the *Death Race 2000* movie.

Negative perception became more widespread in the early eighties when home and arcade games were at their peak. Many parents started blaming video games for the faults of their own children or, more generally, of the younger generation as a whole. One of the most vocal critics was Ms. Ronnie Lamb who was invited to famous TV talk shows where she described how bad video games were for young people by encouraging them to waste money, energy, and valuable time. As a result of her crusade, several small towns in the United States banned video game arcades or stopped opening new ones. Since then, video games have remained in the spotlight.

The front page from a 1983 issue of *Weekly World News*. The headline was dedicated to the sudden death of a teenager who suffered a heart attack while at an arcade. Obviously, video games were accused.

This attitude was not limited to the United States, though, and petitions against video games were raised in many different countries. As early as November 19, 1981, President Marcos of the Philippines banned all video games in his country, giving the population 15 days to destroy or surrender any game console to the army. The negative sentiment was shared in other countries in Southeast Asia. For example, people in Malaysia also asked for the legal ban of video games, claiming, "video games are all about killing, violence, and racism."[1]

In such a heated environment, many people who were unable or unwilling to understand the new media and its unique possibilities would have been more than happy to see video games disappear and would have gladly helped push them into oblivion.

Over-Saturation and Low-Quality Games

In 1982, it was estimated that the US home video game market could absorb up to 60 million cartridges. Unfortunately, that was the number of cartridges Atari alone published throughout the year while Activision was manufacturing between 10 to 15 million and every other company was contributing at least two million, bringing the actual total number to almost 120 million. Obviously, much of this

---

[1] Mr. Martin Khor, Consumers' Association of Penang, Malaysia, as reported in an interview published on local and international newspapers and magazines in early 1983.

huge inventory was not sold and the situation was worsened by a drastic drop in quality for the average title, including those by Atari itself.

The first dramatic example of this new trend occurred in early 1982 when Atari released its own version of the iconic arcade game *Pac-Man*, for which it had recently acquired exclusive rights for home consoles. To capitalize on the *Pac-Man* craze, the game was rushed to market and Ray Kassar finally agreed to give a small royalty to the developer, Todd Frye, as an incentive to work as quickly as possible.[2] The game was programmed in six weeks and released at a $37.50 price point towards the end of March. At that time, Atari's installed user base was estimated to be still less than 10 million units. Nonetheless, Atari manufactured more than 12 million cartridges since they were sure the game would be a system seller and everyone would buy it. Unfortunately, the game was a very poor imitation of the original, bugged by slow animations and an unbearable flickering effect that made the ghost continuously disappear from the screen.

Despite all this, Atari's *Pac-Man* sold seven million units; however, that still left the company with a huge unsold inventory and, more importantly, it disillusioned most VCS owners who started losing faith in the system's actual capabilities.

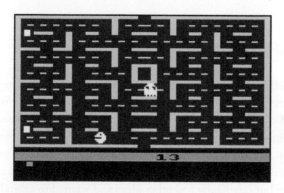

Pac-Man for the Atari 2600. Notice how only one ghost and two power pellets are visible in this screenshot—the others were not displayed in this frame due to flickering. Despite selling seven million units thanks to *Pac-Man* fever, its poor quality tarnished Atari's reputation forever.

Unfortunately, this was only the first among a string of poor games that Atari had in the pipeline. Many soon followed, including an unlikely rendition of Rubik's Cube, ultimately hitting bottom with the infamous *E. T. the Extraterrestrial* game based on the popular movie by Steven Spielberg. In the latter case, even Ray Kassar strongly opposed the project and it was Steve Ross, the head of Warner Communications, who forced it and decided to pay Spielberg $25 million for licensing the game. *E. T.* turned into the worst business deal ever made in video game history and permanently sealed Atari's fate.

---

[2] Todd received $0.10 per cartridge sold.

The fateful deal was signed in July 1982. On July 23, Kassar assigned the project to Howard Scott Warshaw,[3] one of the best young programmers who hadn't yet defected from Atari, with the task of creating the game by September 1 to allow the required manufacturing time and ensure that the game would be on shelves before Christmas. With just a few weeks available, it was no wonder that the game turned out to be a huge disappointment with poor and confusing gameplay, but things were worsened by Ross's decision to manufacture almost five million cartridges. The game sold about 1.5 million, leaving Atari with another huge inventory of unsold cartridges that were buried in a landfill in the New Mexico desert and later destroyed.

Even though companies like Activision and Imagic kept releasing excellent and polished titles, almost all other companies started rushing out weak productions hoping for a quick buck. In a matter of months, the marketplace was cluttered with terrible or even controversial and plainly disgusting titles like *Custer's Revenge* and *Beat 'Em & Eat 'Em"* by Mystique, the first software house to release pornographic games on the Atari 2600.[4] With such an appalling catalogue, it is easy to understand why many people started losing interest in games.

Transitioning to a New Generation

In the early eighties, every issue the industry faced posed new challenges that had to be solved without any historical reference or previous case studies. While the transition from dedicated systems like the Home Pong to cartridge-based systems was natural and straightforward, it wasn't as easy to decide when the next wave of consoles should come out.

As we discussed, Nolan Bushnell would have already launched a new console in the late seventies but Ray Kassar had other ideas and wanted to capitalize as much as possible on the VCS instead. Starting the transition most likely fell on Atari's shoulders. Though Atari was the industry leader, the competition was getting stronger and stronger and something needed to be done; but how could they capitalize on the existing user base? Kassar decided to have two independent systems at the same time—the best selling VCS, now renamed 2600, and the new, more powerful Atari 5200.

Paradoxically, when the 5200 finally came out in November 1982, it had to be pushed by Kassar himself who decided to overrule a petition from Atari's own engineers who were asking to cancel the launch and redesign the console. The 5200 was indeed rushed, both internally (it was basically an Atari 400 computer without any

---

[3] Howard developed hits like *Yar's Revenge* and movie-licensed games like *Raiders of the Lost Ark*.

[4] Atari actually sued Mystique for tarnishing its image. In those days, after Atari lost its legal battles against Activision for producing third-party software, there was no way for hardware manufacturers to control the content of titles published on their systems.

The Atari 5200 Super System. The successor to the VCS was an Atari 400 computer in a different dress. It retailed for $250 and, overall, only 69 games were released before the console was discontinued in March 1984.

new technology whatsoever) and externally, where cheap non-self-centering joysticks made playing arcade style games a real pain. Moreover, the 5200 didn't offer retro compatibility (neither with the 2600 nor with the Atari 400 due to different registry locations in memory) and had only a very limited launching catalogue mostly based on ports, offering no real incentive to existing users to upgrade.

On the other hand, Mattel tried a different route. Instead of producing a completely new system, they decided to do a restyling of their successful Intellivision console to make it look sleeker while also cutting production costs. Released in 1983, the

The Intellivision II was basically a simple restyling of the original and retailed in early 1983 for $150. It was soon discounted to $69 and then discontinued.

Intellivision II featured handy detachable controllers and new add-on peripherals[5] but, unfortunately, construction materials were not as reliable as before; for example, the controllers' side buttons wore out very easily, making the playing experience much more uncomfortable.

Overall, towards the end of 1982 and early 1983, there was not only a proliferation of worthless games, but also a new iteration of consoles that were disappointing for different reasons and, ultimately, delivered experiences that were far below expectations.

Home Computer Wars

As if the preceding problems were not enough to put the video game industry on its knees, the knockout blow was delivered by consoles' "cousins"—the home computers and, more precisely, Commodore.

Having successfully delivered the VIC-20, the first color home computer for less than $300, Commodore's marketing effectively positioned their machine as a "smart" alternative to mere game consoles. The same strategy was adopted and emphasized even more strongly in 1982 with the release of the model that changed the face of home computing: the Commodore 64, or C64 for short. Commodore started retailing its new computer at $595, an already very low price when compared to machines with similar specs like the Apple II, but it soon started cutting its price lower and lower and offering a $100 rebate for anyone who was willing to trade an existing computer or game console for a new C64 in 1983.

Effectively lowering prices while keeping profit margins intact was mainly possible due to Jack Tramiel's aggressive vertical integration approach, but the whole company was actively involved in the process of reducing costs as much as possible. For example, a very hard-working engineering team kept combining and reducing the number of chips required, making the final designs cheaper to manufacture. At the same time, Jack also kept constantly negotiating better prices and deals with vendors for the only peripherals that Commodore was not producing in-house (like printers and disk drives). This was happening very quickly, forcing every computer manufacturer (like Atari, Texas Instruments, Tandy, Apple, etc.) to decide quickly how to behave and react to Commodore's war.

Apple wisely decided to stay out of the fight and ignored Jack's philosophy to "sell to the masses, not to the classes." The latest iteration of the Apple II was

---

[5] New peripherals included a music keyboard and a module to play Atari 2600 games. The Intellivision II tried to prevent unauthorized cartridges to run in an interesting way: by secretly changing the internal exec ROM. As a result of these changes, some Coleco games could not be run anymore. For a proper mechanism to forbid playing unlicensed third-party cartridges, though, players had to wait for Nintendo and its NES launch in 1985.

selling for a much higher price than the C64 while having very similar capabilities, but this strategy, supported by an effective marketing campaign, turned Apple into a company designing "high class" and "cool" products made for people who wanted to differentiate themselves from the generic crowd. While they sold many fewer units than did Commodore, they had a very high profit margin and, ultimately, this unique approach set Apple apart from the competition and worked very well.

Almost every other company instead feared losing too much of their market share and followed Commodore in cutting prices, seriously compromising their profit margins instead. None were as organized as Commodore and able to sustain such a strategy for a long time and they soon had to start selling computers below cost while relying on margins on software sales to make a profit. When Commodore also started reducing the price for its new in-house developed software titles (including both games and utilities) the war was over. In 1983, Commodore was the first computer manufacturer to report $1 billion in sales, seizing the market and leaving all others in the dust.

Casualties

The effects triggered by the combination of these factors were devastating. Basically, all console manufacturers were wiped out in a matter of months and many computer companies and software houses were also forced out of business. Atari racked up a total of more than $500 million in losses in 1983 and Warner ultimately decided to split and sell the company in 1984.

Having the most advanced console didn't save Coleco either, and the company shut down its video game department in 1985 after having lost $258 million. But the most sudden changes happened at Mattel, where, within a two-week period during the spring of 1983, the company went from aggressively hiring game programmers to laying them off. Mattel Electronics posted a $100 million loss in the first half of 1983, and when the total losses added up to $300 million in early 1984, the division was closed permanently.[6]

Not only were hardware manufacturers harmed, but all software houses focusing on game consoles were obviously affected. Many, having just released titles that remained completely unsold with others already in the production pipeline, had to file for bankruptcy. Only the most stable and successful companies were able to survive, often in a much scaled-down structure, thanks to the huge amounts of cash they were able to save from their earlier days. Activision, for example, shifted its focus to

---

[6] The Intellivision rights were sold to a new company, INTV Corp., that kept producing a few games while marketing a restyled version of the console until 1991.

computer games and other software products, and a few years later even changed its name to Mediagenic to emphasize its new global focus.[7]

On the computer side, many of the companies that tried to fight the price war with Commodore were severely affected or even forced out of business. For example, different models that made history during the early days of personal computers quickly lost their appeal and disappeared altogether, like the Texas Instruments TI99/4A. Others slowly faded into oblivion like the Tandy TRS line of computers that, besides being less competitive price-wise, was also confined to the RadioShack electronics stores and couldn't match the market penetration that a more general, non-exclusive approach granted to Commodore machines.

The 1983 crash was particularly devastating in North America (where almost all relevant companies were located), but its effects in other parts of the world, like Europe or Japan, were not as dramatic. In Europe, for example, the market had shifted from consoles to computers too, but European software houses were just beginning their operations at the time. Luckily, they had no unsold backlog catalogue to worry about and had no issues in adapting to the new trends; they started to develop games for computers instead. This approach was also fostered by a growing local computer industry, mostly located in the UK. Video games just changed platforms while remaining the most beloved entertainment activity for kids and teenagers in northern and southern Europe alike.

Games in Japan were having their own independent development too, with new computers and consoles coming out, and the industry was not particularly affected by the crash in the United States. On the contrary, the Japanese gaming scene was actually going to revive the American one in a matter of just a couple years.

---

[7] The original Activision name was restored in December 1992 after the company was bought and completely restructured by a group of investors led by Robert Kotick.

Computers, Computers, Computers

It was not by coincidence that the death of gaming consoles happened together with the rise of the home computers. So it shouldn't be a surprise that different console manufacturers tried a last, dramatic attempt to reverse their fortunes by shifting to the new market as quickly as possible.

The most notable examples were from Mattel and Coleco. In June 1983, Mattel Electronics released a Z-80-based system named Aquarius for $160. Unfortunately, it was "too little, too late"[8] and while a more powerful version named Aquarius II was ready for release soon after, the very poor sales of the first model weren't able to save the Intellivision maker or justify the marketing of yet another model.

Coleco, on the other hand, had more ambitious plans. The Adam computer was marketed as a powerful and complete system, able to challenge any other home computer on the market, exactly like the ColecoVision did for consoles. The Adam was offered either as a docking-bay unit to transform the ColecoVision into a real computer or as a stand-alone machine at $725. It was bundled with a cassette player/recorder, a printer, and useful software like a word processor.

The Aquarius home computer didn't save Mattel Electronics and was discontinued a few months after its release.

---

[8] Mattel's own programmers, sadly, described it as "the computer for the seventies."

The Adam. Turning the ColecoVision into a computer was potentially a great idea, but the execution fell short and produced one of the most unreliable computers ever.

The emergency arising from the new market conditions pushed Coleco to rush the project and its design, with the result that the final computer was to be remembered as one of the buggiest and most unreliable machines in history. For example, when powered up, the machine emitted a magnetic pulse strong enough to erase any tape left inside. Also, the printer was prone to breaking easily and this actually halted the whole system because the power-up switch was located on the printer itself. In the end, about 60% of all Adams were returned to stores as defective. Slashing the price to $300 didn't save either the ill-fated computer or its maker as hoped, but actually worsened its situation.

There was also another company actively involved in both consoles and computers: Atari. Since 1979, Atari had started manufacturing a string of 8-bit-based home computers. They were originally meant to compete with Apple, and many different models followed throughout the years to compete with the new generations of 8-bit systems like the TI99/4A, VIC-20, and C64. Unfortunately, most of them had little or no success, starting from the first models. The Atari 400 was extremely limited feature-wise while the 800 never really caught fire because Atari computers were always priced higher than those of its competitors. And the whole Atari brand was always associated with gaming consoles, even when talking about "computers."[9] Nonetheless, one of their last models in the 8-bit series was particularly well designed and met with relatively good success: the Atari 800XL.

---

[9] Recall that VCS stands for Video Computer System, a name that was sure to attract people's attention when the whole notion of home computers was foreign to most people. In the early eighties, though, it might have backfired by making Atari's actual computers look like gaming consoles to the inexperienced buyer.

Atari 800XL

The Atari 800XL was released in 1983 to compete head to head with the C64 and it was the best computer in the Atari line so far—it had 64K RAM, a built in BASIC language, and it was designed around a 6502 CPU clocked at 1.79 MHz.[10] Additionally, it had custom chips to handle graphics (sprites, collision detection, etc.) and input/output operations that made it a very fast and performance-oriented machine able to handle games requiring complex mathematical operations such as *Rescue on Fractalus!*.

The 800XL was a truly pioneering machine and it developed new solutions that became standard in the following years. The MS-DOS specification to format PC floppy disks, for example, was nothing more than the Atari DOS format, and USB connections still used now are an evolution of the original Atari serial, the interface used to connect Atari peripherals.

The Atari 800XL was a groundbreaking machine that implemented several technical ideas that were later adopted in different computers. Unfortunately, its high price point together with a relatively late launch hampered its success.

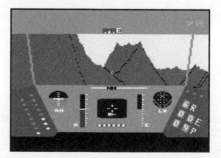

Rescue on Fractalus!, developed by LucasFilm and published by Activision in 1985, was one of the most representative titles for the 800XL, featuring not only an immersive world but also showing the technical prowess of the system. The game was ported to other computers, but this remained the reference and definitive version.

---

[10] By comparison, the clock on the Commodore 64 was running at only 1 MHz.

Commodore 64

No other computer can be considered as representative of a whole technological era as the Commodore 64 was for the early and mid-eighties.

What set it apart from all other systems of the time was that the C64 was the only home computer able to gain an audience worldwide.[11] While other systems could also be very successful in specific regions and could actually challenge the C64's dominance, like the ZX Spectrum in the UK or the MSX in Japan, they failed to gain a meaningful share in other markets, reducing their global impact and significance.

The C64 was impressive at the time of its release for its multimedia qualities. Graphics and audio were handled by the VIC-II and SID chips, respectively, allowing for 16 colors and eight sprites on-screen while a beautiful three-channel audio synthesizer took care of the music and could also simulate the human voice without any additional hardware. All of this, together with a starting price that was much lower than that of several competitors, made it the most popular choice. Excellent first- and third-party software didn't take long to arrive: word processors, spreadsheets (like Microsoft's Multiplan), and games from Activision, Infocom, Electronic Arts, Cinemaware, Epyx, and Commodore itself quickly built a truly enviable catalogue.

Among non-gaming applications, Magic Desk, released in 1983, was particularly interesting as it helped place the C64 into a more "serious" perspective compared to

The Commodore 64, the most popular home computer in history. When released in 1982 for $595, production costs amounted to $130, which were later slashed to around $50 thanks to Commodore's efforts in vertical integration, negotiation, and engineering skills. It's clear then how Commodore could comfortably reduce prices down to $200 while maintaining excellent profits and wiping out most of the competition from the market.

---

[11] According to Commodore's 1993 Annual Report, the C64 sold around 17 million units between 1982 and 1993. These, together with the 4.5 million sales of the backward-compatible Commodore 128, led many analysts to conclude that the C64 was the first computer platform to effectively sell more than 20 million units worldwide.

Andrew Spencer's *International Soccer*, one of the in-house titles developed by Commodore and released in 1983. At the time, this was by far the best soccer game ever seen on a TV screen apart from the real thing.

its early days. It was a completely graphical user interface (GUI)-driven application incorporating a word processor, and all of the commands needed to create, save, and delete new documents were made executable by pointing a hand-shaped cursor towards the appropriate icon.

Magic Desk was released around the same time as the first full-fledged icon-based operating systems (OS) from Apple[12] and the C64 would soon have its own new GUI-based OS, the Graphical Environment Operating System (GEOS), for which several business applications were developed (see the figure on the top of page 84).

Overall, more than 20,000 games and applications were developed and the C64's popularity forced Commodore to resume its production by public demand several times in the late eighties before finally discontinuing it in 1992.

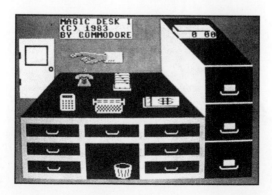

Magic Desk, developed in-house by Commodore, was a pioneering effort in defining new icon-driven environments.

---

[12] The Apple Lisa, the first computer with a full icon-based OS, was released in 1983 at a price of $9,995.

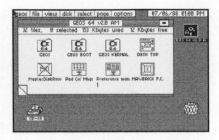

Developed by Berkeley Softworks and released in 1986, the GEOS made the C64 comparable to the Apple Mac, at a fraction of the price.

ZX Spectrum

Clive Sinclair saw the culmination of his research in affordable home computers with the ZX Spectrum, of which two different versions (16K and 48K RAM) were released in April 1982.

Though not a multimedia powerhouse by any means,[13] the built-in Sinclair BASIC language and overall huge improvements from the previously-pioneering ZX81 made this machine a much beloved model in the hands of hobbyists and aspiring programmers. It played a fundamental role in starting and fostering the early development of the UK gaming industry.

Many new companies started to write software and, most importantly, games for the new machine: Bug-Byte, Mikro-Gen, Quicksilva, Imagine, Ocean, and Ultimate became common household names, and several magazines dedicated to reviewing

The original ZX Spectrum, the most well-known and best selling British home computer. More than 12,000 games were programmed for it. It used a Z-80A chip running at 3.54 MHz and had a resolution of 256 × 192 pixels.

---

[13] The Spectrum offered only seven colors (with dark and bright variations) plus black, and provided only a simple BEEP command for controlling pitch and duration of one audio channel.

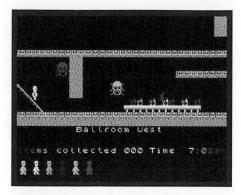

Released in 1984 by Software Projects, *Jet Set Willy* was the follow-up to an earlier success named *Manic Miner*. The object was to follow Willy in collecting 83 objects spread all around his huge manor while avoiding a multitude of traps before he could finally have a well-deserved rest. An extremely difficult, unforgiving, but fascinating quest, *Jet Set Willy* spawned countless clones and successfully redefined the platforming genre on home computers.

and discussing the new gaming culture cropped up all around. Indeed, the results came quickly and iconic figures from games like *Jet Set Willy* by Matthew Smith or technical marvels like Ultimate's *Knight Lore* captivated the imaginations of an entire generation of gamers.

Overall, the ZX Spectrum was a great computer that is still remembered fondly by many. It was extremely successful across Europe, where it shaped the nascent computer game industry, but it didn't succeed in conquering the North American or other markets where the name Sinclair didn't have a strong enough tradition upon which to build.

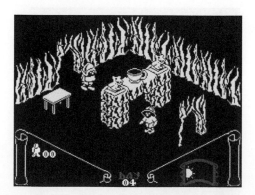

Knight Lore (1984) by Chris and Tim Stamper, the founders of Ultimate and, later, Rare. Thanks to their Filmation engine, an in-house-developed technology, *Knight Lore* was a true marvel that amazed all gaming enthusiasts with its spectacular isometric perspective and that set a new bar in exploratory arcade/adventure games. In the game, an explorer named Sabreman was under a spell that, at night, transformed him into a werewolf. His only hope was to find a powerful wizard within 40 days and nights to lift the curse and save him.

BBC Micro

Sinclair's machines would not remain unchallenged for long. A former Sinclair engineer, Chris Curry, together with an Austrian friend named Hermann Hauser, cofounded a new competing company called Acorn Computers in 1978. After the first experiments, the company took off in 1981 thanks to winning the BBC's Computer Literacy Project call for proposals. Two models were released in late 1981: the BBC

The BBC Micro, the most successful home computer on the educational scene with 1.5 million units sold, ran a 6502A CPU clocked at 2 MHz.

The space trading simulation *Elite*, programmed by Dave Braben and Ian Bell in 1984, was the best game for the BBC Micro and was considered to be a "system seller." It was a ground-breaking game where players were free to play in any way they liked—as an honest trader or as a space pirate, for example—while exploring a vast universe.

I WAS A TEENAGE ZOMBIE!

MIDWESTERN YOUTH TELLS HOW INFOCOM DEPROGRAMMING BROUGHT HIM BACK FROM A LIVING DEATH.

PLAYER'S GUIDE TO PROGRAMMABLE VIDEOGAMES

electronic GAMES

Videogames · Computer Games · Stand-Alone Games · Arcades

Winter $2.95

CAN ASTEROIDS CONQUER SPACE INVADERS?

ATTACK OF THE CHESS ROBOTS

INSIDE THE TRS-80 COLOR COMPUTER

STRATEGY SESSION: SPACE INVADERS & BREAKOUT—TRICKS TO WIN!

TOUCHDOWN! YOU'RE THE COACH WITH ELECTRONIC FOOTBALL

HOLIDAY GIFT GIVING FOR GAMERS

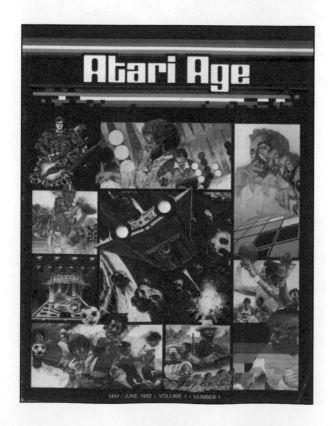

Atari Age

MAY / JUNE 1982 • VOLUME 1 • NUMBER 1

VIDEO GAMES

FEBRUARY 1983
US $2.95
Canada $3.25

Exclusive:
The Godfather
of Video Games &
Marty Ingles
Have Their Say

WHAT'S NEW
FOR '83

The Games
Network

Super
Pac-Man

Saviour One

The Atari 5200

3-D Everything

PLUS
Our Dream Machine

SPECIAL 27-PAGE HOME COMPUTER SECTION

NINTENDO POWER

July/August 1988 $3.50

Super Mario 2
20-Page Spectacular

Zelda — Second Quest
In-Depth Review

Baseball Roundup

Over 50 Pro Tips

Free
Poster Inside

Nintendo THE SOURCE FOR NES PLAYERS STRAIGHT FROM THE PROS

Model A and Model B with 16 KB and 32 KB RAM, respectively, with more models to come in the following years.

BBC's educational program made Acorn's latest creation a common tool in all British schools and its success was so great that it was used later in similar programs in other Commonwealth countries, such as India, throughout the eighties.

Though it was not originally meant to play games, the BBC Micro would have a relevant role in the industry, mostly thanks to an extremely influential and ground-breaking game, *Elite*, which was first programmed on this system before being ported to many others and inspiring countless titles up to this very day.

Acorn was sold to Olivetti in 1985 but the BBC Micro was produced, in different iterations, until 1994.

Amstrad CPC

Sinclair and Acorn were not the only players on the British home computer scene, though, and Amstrad, an electronics company founded in 1968 by Alan Sugar, soon played a major role. The Color Personal Computer (CPC) line of computers was launched in 1984 and soon gathered a large following, mostly in the UK and central Europe.

Games on the CPC were quite varied and, in the mid-eighties, most games in Europe were ported to all of the three main platforms of the time: the C64, the ZX Spectrum, and the CPC. Amstrad also bought Sinclair in 1986, continuing the Spectrum line with different iterations that, unfortunately, were not able to match the machine's early successes. The CPC line was ultimately discontinued in 1990 after an attempt to enter the video game market directly with a computer-turned-console model, the GX4000, that didn't catch much attention.

The Z-80 powered CPC 464, the first model in the CPC line. It had 64 KB RAM and an internal cassette deck.

MSX

MSX was the Japanese answer to American and European home computers. Actually, it was not just a "computer" but a full standard—spanning hardware and software—and it was designed so that different manufacturers would produce compatible machines on a common architecture.

Starting from mid-1983, several Japanese and Korean electronics companies, such as Sony, Sharp, JVC, Canon, Toshiba, Sanyo, and Daewoo, started developing MSX computers. Despite being strongly supported by Microsoft Japan from the very beginning,[14] MSX didn't really succeed in developing a following in the western

A MSX model by Philips. MSX computers were mounting a Z-80 and had different amounts of RAM, from 16 KB and upwards. The last MSX model, the MSXTurboR, was discontinued in 1995.

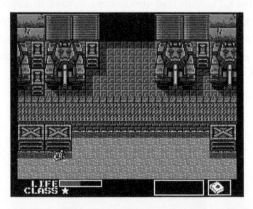

The beginning of a new, epic adventure: the first *Metal Gear* game by Hideo Kojima, published in 1987. Though some earlier games did incorporate a stealth-based mechanic, it was perfected here and became the main game focus, starting a whole new genre.

---

[14] Kazuhiko Nishi, VP of Microsoft Japan and Director at ASCII Corporation, was responsible for the initial standard proposal. According to an interview in 2001, as reported on www.msx.org, Mr. Nishi explained that the "MSX" acronym meant "machines with software exchangeability," though different alternative meanings have been provided through the years.

world, where the market was already crowded. However, it became a very popular choice in countries like Japan and South Korea. Overall, MSX computers sold about five million units worldwide.

Despite its limited geographical relevance, the MSX played an important role in fostering the gaming industry in Japan, somewhat like the ZX Spectrum did in the UK. In fact, some of today's most beloved franchises created by Japanese developers, like *Metal Gear*, *Bomberman*, and *Puyo Puyo*, were actually created on MSX computers first before being ported to other systems.

Apple II

Even though Apple refused to join the on-going price war and maintained a steep price tag on its models, the different iterations of the Apple II were still able to play an important role across the gaming scene, especially in North America where it often turned out to be the tool of choice by many talented developers.

The Apple IIe, with 64 KB of RAM and the ability to display both lowercase and uppercase letters, was released in 1983 (see the figure on the top of page 90) and it was followed by the IIc in 1984, a compact and portable version that doubled the available RAM.

Overall, including the 16-bit Apple IIGS released in 1986, the Apple II series was an "all-arounder," equally at ease in the office, in a research facility, and at home. It ended up selling between five and six million units, leaving a mark in the memories of many.

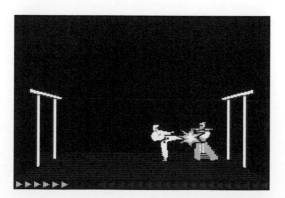

Several seminal games, like Jordan Mechner's *Karateka* (1984), a side-scroller action game that served as a basis for the later *Prince of Persia*, were originally conceived on the Apple II.

The IIe was the Apple II model with the longest lifespan and it was produced until 1993.

And What about the IBM PC?

The first IBM PC, the model 5150, was released on August 12, 1981, mounting an Intel 8088 processor clocked at 4.77 MHz. This was a business-oriented machine

The first IBM PC ever released, the model 5150. In 1982, 200,000 units were sold, but not with the intention of playing games.

with extremely limited audio and graphical capabilities that was targeted to office use only. It also had a retail price much higher than any of the home computers of the time, even before Commodore started its savage price war: $1,565 without monitor and floppy disk.

Games started being developed a bit more seriously from 1984 onwards with the release of the AT series, but PC games still had a long way to go before matching the multimedia capabilities of other home computers; ultimately, in the early nineties, this was accomplished.

Atari and Commodore:
from Here, Where?

• • • • • • • • • • • • •

Both Atari and Commodore played a major role in the crash of 1983, albeit for completely different reasons, and ended up in two very different positions. Atari racked up more than $500 million in losses and struggled to remain in business. One possible move was to push another, more powerful, console to address the various complaints that caused the Atari 5200's failure. The design of the Atari 7800 started in 1983 and the machine was released in mid-1984 with a price tag of $140 and the nearly impossible task of reviving a collapsing market.

At about the same time that the 7800 was ready to be shipped, Warner management decided to split Atari into two distinct branches so that they could eventually be sold more easily: Atari Games, the arcade division, and the Atari Consumer Division, which included the home computing and consoles products.

The Atari 7800 Pro System was by far the best console Atari had ever released up to that time. It was retro compatible with the 2600, had proper controllers, and its 6502-based architecture was enhanced by a dedicated graphic chip named MARIA that was able to handle up to 100 objects on screen while showcasing 25 different colors chosen from a palette of 256.

Commodore, on the other hand, was the clear winner in the business war started by Jack Tramiel and was in a truly enviable position, having just passed the $1 billion mark in sales thanks to the overwhelming success of the C64. Then something unexpected happened, and internal politics took its toll.

At the beginning of 1984, Tramiel wanted his sons to work with him in the family business, but his hopes most likely encountered Irving Gould's disapproval. Gould wanted a different leadership to drive the company to even higher successes. Though it's not clear what happened exactly, in January, Jack suddenly quit the company he founded and in July of the same year he bought the Atari Consumer Division, renaming it Atari Corp.

Jack and his son Sam started restructuring Atari from the ground up with the consequence that even the newly launched 7800 console was withdrawn from the market to re-discuss licensing and manufacturing deals. Unfortunately for Atari, the 7800 was re-released only two years later when the market was already in other steady hands.

Jack's move left Commodore without clear leadership and problems started to surface quickly. Replicating the C64's success was harder than anyone thought—something that Atari had just experienced after the tremendous success of its 2600. The new models introduced in 1984, the Commodore 16 and the Plus/4, were total commercial failures and were soon discontinued. Commodore had to find a new hit somewhere else and, indeed, they found it in a small company named Amiga Corporation.

Amiga Corporation [15] was founded by ex-Atari employees, including Jay Miner (1932–1994), one of the original designers responsible for the custom chips in the Atari VCS. In 1982, Amiga started working on a new gaming console, codenamed

The short-lived Commodore Plus/4. Having four built-in applications including a spreadsheet editor and word processor was not what customers really wanted and people simply kept buying the C64 instead, leaving this new machine on the shelves.

---

[15] The company's original name was actually Hi-Toro, but it was soon changed to Amiga Corporation.

Lorraine, which was based on the Motorola 68000 processor.[16] After a first round of funding by local venture capital firms, Atari itself funded the company with $500,000 in exchange for one year of exclusive rights for any design the company may have created. Commodore bought the whole start-up in 1984 for $25 million and returned the $500,000 check to Atari to free the Lorraine team from any former ties with the competition.

Meanwhile, back at Atari, Jack didn't waste time; he fired many of the existing executives who drove the once successful company into the ground and brought over several of his trusted "Commodorians," both executives and engineers, who were accustomed to his "religious" way of doing business. The goal was to bring the company back to profitability by cutting costs while developing a new, powerful home computer system.

This swap of talent, together with the previously Atari-funded Amiga Corporation being acquired by Commodore, triggered a series of lawsuits and countersuits between the two companies involving the infringement of trade and industry secrets that were ultimately settled out of court in 1987. The net result, though, was that the next generation of powerful home computers was finally in the works.

---

[16] The 68000 was a powerful 16-bit CPU first introduced in 1979 and still in use today.

Nintendo Gives Consoles an Extra Life: the NES, ROB, and *Super Mario*

• •

As discussed previously, Nintendo released the Famicom in Japan with instant success in 1983. After a first failed attempt to export it to the United States through Atari, Nintendo's president Hiroshi Yamauchi felt that the time was finally right to try again in 1985 through direct distribution (thanks to Nintendo's own American branch led by his son-in-law, Minoru Arakawa). Market conditions were still quite difficult, though. Video games were considered to be dead and Arakawa and his team had to be extremely cautious about their every move. And they were—they took a lot of precautions in differentiating their product from the old competition while trying to avoid the main problems that plagued the previous generation: namely, an overflow of poor quality games.

The first necessity was to change the name of the console and to present it as something different. The words "video game" had to be absolutely avoided and the word "computer" wasn't favorable any more because it could have recalled Atari's Video Computer System. The Famicom was then renamed Nintendo Entertainment System, or NES, and marketed as something completely original, not just as a new gaming console. At launch, the NES featured a light gun and a small robot called ROB[17] that could perform simple tasks like running and carrying small objects.

The Famicom, rebranded as the Nintendo Entertainment System for its North American debut. Besides great games, the NES also made popular a new type of controller: the D-Pad. First introduced in Nintendo's early handheld electronic games, it overtook all previous joystick/paddle approaches and became the new standard control scheme.

---

[17] The Robot Operating Buddy was one of the countless projects that Nintendo's lead engineer Gunpei Yokoi (1941–1997) worked on over the years.

ROB was actually quite helpful in delivering the new message and the NES started to effectively attract both the public's and retailers' interest as a new "cool robot game." One by one, new market testing locations were slowly opened, starting in New York on October 18, 1985, before the nationwide American launch in February 1986.

As noted, in addition to a proper marketing strategy, Nintendo was particularly concerned about the quality of the games available on its system. It wasn't by chance that the NES was launched with a very strong lineup of 18 titles, including *Duck Hunt* and *Donkey Kong Jr.*, which were soon followed by *Super Mario Bros.* *Super Mario* was especially important as it quickly surged to an iconic status, taking over *Pac-Man*'s place in the collective imagination to represent a new breed of video games that featured not only better graphics and sound, but also more complex adventures set in larger, more interactive worlds.

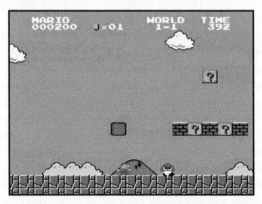

The original *Super Mario Bros.* (1986): platform games redefined into a huge, varied world. Designed by the creative genius of Shigeru Miyamoto, it was not only the biggest, longest, and most complex game ever made but also one of the first action games that actually ended once the story (saving the princess) was over.[18] Yet it also offered a great replay value thanks to many hidden areas and secrets to be discovered. Mario soon became the new icon for video games, taking over *Pac-Man*'s legacy by starting a franchise where each new game in the series was received with enthusiasm by countless fans worldwide.

Overall, Nintendo put a lot of effort into setting a very high bar and, to achieve a similar standard from third-party developers, it decided to enforce a strict quality policy on all titles that were going to be released on its platform: no developer was allowed to release more than five titles per year. The system was even able to automatically halt unauthorized cartridges from running thanks to a specific chip, the 10NES, which implemented a security system that only official cartridges could unlock. These measures were especially important to avoid the glut of very poor titles that characterized the totally uncontrolled marketplace of the previous generation.

---

[18] The first game of this kind was Epyx's *Impossible Mission*, released in 1983, which is reviewed in the Games That Pushed Boundaries section.

The Nintendo Seal of Quality soon became a way for buyers to trust Nintendo and the games that were published on the NES and any subsequent console.

Accordingly, a developer willing to release a game on the NES had to submit it to Nintendo for approval first, which was eventually granted through a "Seal of Quality" and then the manufactured cartridge had to incorporate the proper key to unlock the 10NES security system, provided by Nintendo itself.

In addition to these new rules, Nintendo wasn't really keen to distribute any sort of technical documentation, and life for third-party developers who wanted to release titles for the new system was far from easy. Many actually had to reverse engineer the console to understand how it worked. This practice became so widespread that quite a few people had the impression that Nintendo was doing this on purpose and the "reverse engineering" task was actually an "entrance" test to probe the skills of its prospective licensees and see whether they were smart enough to deliver high quality games. This was also the case for companies like Rare, founded by Chris and Tim Stamper,[19] which released fundamental titles for Nintendo's consoles for years to come, including games such as *Donkey Kong Country* (1994, on the SNES) and *GoldenEye 007* (1997, on the Nintendo 64).

Overall, before being discontinued in 1995, the NES ended up selling 61.91 million units worldwide and became one of the most significant successes in the history of video games.

---

[19] These were the same men who had previously founded Ultimate and developed some of the best games ever on the ZX Spectrum. Rare was founded to keep developing games independently once Ultimate was bought by US Gold in 1985.

New Competition:
the Sega Master System

• • • • • • • • • • • • • • • • •

Thanks to NES's success, by 1986 it was clear the video game craze wasn't dead and Atari finally decided to re-release its 7800 ProSystem. Unfortunately, having shifted its focus to home computers didn't help the new Atari company regain ground on the console scene, and despite the merits of the 7800, the two-year-old machine failed to conquer a significant market share.[20]

New, and more dangerous, competition came instead from the same company that relased the SG-1000 in Japan at the same time Nintendo launched the Famicom: Sega. On October 20, 1985, Sega released a new console in Japan named Mark III while North American and European launches followed in mid-1986 and 1987, respectively, with a $200 price tag. The console was sold in two different packages: the Sega Base System and the Sega Master System, which included a light gun in addition to the standard console. The latter was by far the more common of the two and, ultimately, Sega decided to rebrand the console according to the new, more popular name. While Nintendo's dominance on the North American and Japanese markets was practically impossible to challenge at this time, the Master System found fertile ground in other regions like Europe and South America where it was able to quickly gather a strong following that pushed most of its overall 13 million unit sales.

The Sega Master System. Based on a Z-80 CPU, it was the only console able to compete with the NES in the mid-eighties, especially in Europe, and ended up selling about 13 million units.

---

[20] The 7800 ended up selling about four million units and, in contrast to the 2600, had a small but high-quality catalogue of games featuring about 60 titles.

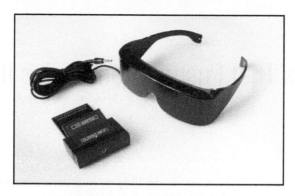

Sega's 3D glasses. An LCD shutter made each lense opaque in sync with the image on screen to create a 3D stereoscopic effect. Only eight games were made compatible with this system but these included beloved arcade classics such as *Out Run* and *Zaxxon*.

Like the NES before it, the Master System tried to capture the public's attention by offering interesting add-ons, such as different types of controllers (including a remote/wireless one) and even a set of 3D glasses. Unfortunately, Sega wasn't able to secure proper third-party support from many American developers and its games failed to deliver iconic figures like Super Mario or Donkey Kong.[21] Across its 300+ games catalogue, only a few were really able to attract worldwide attention, most notably *Phantasy Star*, which spawned a successful franchise and paved the way to many Japanese RPGs.

Internally developed by Sega with Rieko Kodama and Yuji Naka as lead designer and programmer, respectively, *Phantasy Star* was an adventure RPG first released in Japan during December 1987. Thanks to a young but strong female main character (an unusual choice at the time), extensive world maps with towns and dungeons, random enemy encounters, turn-based battles, and an alternating 2D and first-person perspective, it was one of the first groundbreaking Japanese RPGs that set a standard for many more games to come.

---

[21] Sega's most iconic character, Sonic the Hedgehog, wasn't released until 1991.

Games That Pushed Boundaries II

• •

Having analyzed the developments in the industry and the main systems that were popular in the early to mid-eighties, let's turn our attention to some of the most influential arcade and 8-bit games developed during this time.

Football Manager (1982, Addictive Games)

Developed in BASIC first on the TRS-80 and then ported to Sinclair's ZX-81 and the new ZX Spectrum for proper commercial distribution, *Football Manager* was an instant success. It granted its author, Kevin Toms, fame and fortune—every football fan always dreamed of being able to set up his favorite team in the way he wanted, and finally he had a virtual chance to do so. The game was also notable for fully exploiting all features of the ZX Spectrum's built-in BASIC language. Even its liabilities, like its slow speed, were turned into strengths: watching the highlights of your own game and then waiting for the other league results to be slowly generated one by one was indeed a clever way to add tension and suspense to the whole virtual experience.

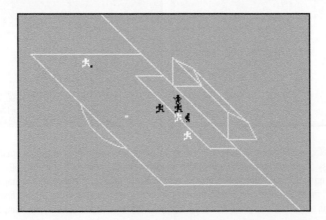

A screenshot from the ZX Spectrum version of *Football Manager*. It was the first version of the game to feature simple graphic sequences representing the match highlights; after a few seconds of semi-random action on the screen, a footballer would eventually shoot towards the goal.

After having sold extremely well on the ZX Spectrum (more than 300,000 copies with an installed user base of about four million), *Football Manager* was soon ported to many other computers in the following years and started the sports management simulation genre that has remained popular ever since.

Pole Position (1982, Atari)

After the first pioneering attempt to provide a somewhat realistic experience with *Night Driver*, Atari was ready to redefine the driving genre with *Pole Position*. A proper circuit, qualifying laps, shifting gears, and, most importantly, a rudimentary but well-implemented physics system truly gave players a realistic feeling of speed. Every turn had to be properly planned by setting the right speed and trajectory and the player had to avoid other cars because a simple collision would cause an explosion and waste precious time.

Pole Position soon became so popular that it was ported on many different systems, both computers (Atari, Commodore 64, VIC-20, ZXSpectrum, and TI99/4A) and consoles (Atari 2600 and 5200, Intellivision, and Vectrex). A sequel, *Pole Position II*, featuring more circuits was also released in 1983.

Pole Position, with its challenging and addictive gameplay, could be regarded as the first great driving game, paving the way for all other simulations to come.

Atic Atac (1983, Ultimate)

Basically a ZX Spectrum exclusive (a porting to BBC Micro was developed in 1985 but didn't receive much attention), *Atic Atac* was the second game developed by Chris and Tim Stamper. It marked the beginning of their graphical adventure software (GAS) series, which affected not only the ZX Spectrum game scene but also the whole industry.

Atic Atac was a mind-blowing game when released in 1983 thanks to its smooth and arcade-quality graphics. Its creepy settings and exciting action made it one of the very first examples of survival/horror games. Note also the humorous half-eaten chicken that represented players' health—food items were spread across the rooms to replenish it.

The game, set in a haunted manor, was unique for its top-down camera perspective, for the many different enemies (from simple minions and ghosts to Dracula and Frankenstein), and for giving players a choice of character. That choice—a knight, a wizard, or a serf—was not only aesthetic but affected the gameplay because each character had access to a specific shortcut within the castle, adding more variety and replay value to the whole experience.

The huge castle map together with the cute, funny, and smoothly-animated sprites made the quest for finding the main gate key and escaping alive a truly entertaining game that is still remembered today.

One on One (1983, Electronic Arts)

While Mattel started using official "generic" licenses for its sport games, like NBA basketball, NASL soccer, and NFL football, as early as 1979, it was Electronic Arts, with *One on One: Dr. J vs. Larry Bird*, that was first to exploit the likes of specific, real athletes for a video game.[22] Designed by Eric Hammond and released first on the Atari 8-bit and Apple II computers (the Commodore 64 and ColecoVision versions followed in 1984 with a few more ports released in 1987, including an Atari 7800 cartridge), this game depicted the two NBA stars, Julius Erving and Larry Bird, in

---

[22] In 1980, Sears released the Atari-developed *Championship Soccer* for the Atari VCS, which was re-released by Atari itself one year later as *Pelé's Soccer*. While that was the first time a sports game bore the name of a real athlete, there was no attempt to recreate the actual likeness and skills of the star in the game and the license worked simply as an endorsement and marketing tool. *Pelé's Soccer* was also notable for being the first soccer game to show a top-down camera view—a perspective that was perfected years later in games such as *Kick Off* and *Microprose Soccer*.

Dr. J vs. Larry Bird (here in the Apple II version) started a whole new trend and opened up new business opportunities.

a one-on-one challenge that offered very fast and exciting gameplay for one or two players. Three-pointers, slam dunks, and free throws were all included, making this the most spectacular basketball game in its day. For the first time, kids could play a game and really have the "feeling" that they were one of their sporting heroes.

Dragon's Lair (1983, Cinematronics)

At a time when video game graphics could be described as "cute" at best, *Dragon's Lair* took the gaming scene by storm. It was the first laser disk-based game to be released in the arcades and it literally put players into an animated movie. Masterfully drawn by Don Bluth, Dirk the Daring had to save the beautiful Daphne from the evil dragon Singe. Gameplay wise, it was actually very simple: just a series of branching points handled by quick time events. Nonetheless, the novelty of being an integral part of an "interactive movie" made *Dragon's Lair* a true classic and granted it an everlasting popularity that no other laser disk game could achieve.

Leading Dirk through the many dangers of Singe's castle was a fascinating, though expensive (each play required $0.50, while most other games of the time were playable with only a quarter), journey.

Mario Bros. (1983, Nintendo)

Designed by Shigeru Miyamoto and produced by Gunpei Yokoi, this is the game that took Jumpman from *Donkey Kong*, renamed him Mario, and gave him an Italian nationality, a job as a plumber, and a brother named Luigi.

First released in the arcades in 1983, the game was structured as an apparently simple platformer. Players had to disinfest a sewer from cute pests like turtles and crabs, which had to be turned upside-down by hitting them from the lower platform first before they could be kicked out of the screen. The most notable aspect of the game, though, was the two-player mode with both Mario and Luigi joining the action. Here the players, while still competing between themselves for the high score, had to help each other to eliminate all of the enemies and proceed through as many levels as possible. This mixed cooperative and competitive action was a very innovative gameplay element that gave *Mario Bros.* a lot of replay value and long-lasting appeal.

From the arcades, *Mario Bros.* was soon ported to the NES and then licensed to many 8-bit home computers, spreading the popularity of its main characters.

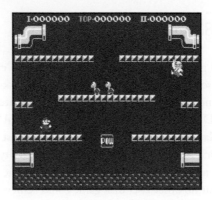

Mario and Luigi in action. Turtles couldn't be taken head-on but had to be turned upside-down by hitting them from the platform below.

M.U.L.E. (1983, Electronic Arts)

M.U.L.E. was an extremely original game first developed for the Atari 8-bit and the Commodore 64 computers by Dan Bunten. The game involved a four-player mission to colonize an alien planet.[23] The title, meaning Multiple Use Labor Element, referred to the robot mules that were used throughout the game to gather different resources (food, ore, energy, and a rare, planet-specific mineral called "crystite"). The game was turn-based with each turn being affected by every resource in a player's possession.

---

[23] All four players could play at the same keyboard or up to three could have been handled by the AI.

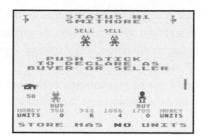

The trading phase of *M.U.L.E,* where players could bargain with each other to obtain the resources they needed most.

For example, a lack of food would allow less time to perform tasks, low energy could hinder the player from extracting resources from the land, and so on. What made this game unique, though, was its clever, yet simple, economic model based on supply/demand principles where players could sell goods to each other and improve their own productivity or even collude to damage other players.

M.U.L.E. was also notable for being one of the first titles to implement a balancing system. While there were both good and bad random events that could affect players, favorable events would not happen to the leading colonizer and bad ones could not be triggered for the trailing player, making for a more even and exciting competition.

Impossible Mission (1983, Epyx)

Impossible Mission, designed by Dennis Caswell, was first released on the C64 before being ported to many other systems (including consoles such as the NES, Atari 7800, and Sega Master System). *Impossible Mission* was one of the games that pushed the technical capabilities of 8-bit computers to new heights—colorful graphics, smooth animations, and digitized speech made many players' jaws drop in wonder.

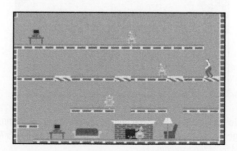

Ask anyone who played this game back in the day and most likely they will still remember Atombender's mean greetings at the beginning of the game, "Another visitor! Stay a while, staaaay FOREVER!" It was one of the truly defining moments of 8-bit gaming.

With the players as secret agents on a mission to infiltrate the hidden base of Professor Elvin Atombender and fight off his evil plans, the gameplay consisted of a clever mix of exploration, platforming, stealth action, and puzzle-solving to unlock the password codes needed to access the Professor's secret control room.

Impossible Mission should also be remembered as the very first action/platformer game that actually ended once the mission was successfully accomplished.

Karate Champ (1984, Data East)

Martial arts in general and karate in particular saw a big boost in popularity in 1984 thanks to blockbuster movies like *Karate Kid*, with the consequence that many new fighting games started to be designed and released in the arcades.

While not the first fighting game to be released,[24] *Karate Champ* was the first one to become very popular and successful. It featured two karateka who had to fight each other in stages of two rounds each and included a good variety of moves, like reverse round-house kicks and somersaults, thanks to an effective dual joystick control system (no buttons were present). Timing and proper positioning were essential for blocking and delivering the right strikes to score the two points needed to win the match and advance to the next stage.

The original, arcade version of *Karate Champ*. The game was ported to the Commodore 64, Apple II, and NES and inspired a new generation of successful karate-based games like Epyx's *International Karate* and Melbourne House's *The Way of the Exploding Fist*.

---

[24] Sega's *Heavyweight Champ* was released in 1976.

Notably too, bonus stages were present where, for example, the player had to fight a bull or break objects to get extra points.

Lords of Midnight (1984, Beyond Software)

Developed by Mike Singleton and inspired by Tolkien's *Lord of the Rings* saga, *Lords of Midnight* was by far one of the most original and captivating turn-based adventure RPG of the eighties. The game began with the player controlling a group of four warriors headed by Luxor the Moonprince, and it was possible to recruit more characters and armies while traveling across the incredibly vast game world in the attempt to defeat the evil forces invading the land of Midnight.

What made the game extremely appealing were its magical atmosphere (the graphics featured forests, hills, lakes, towns, and more) as well as the possibility of allowing different and independent playing strategies. For example, the player could decide to amass a huge army and face the evil Doomdark and his forces directly, or to embark on a more solitary mission to find and destroy the Ice Crown, from which the evil lord was gaining his strength and powers.

Lords of Midnight became an instant classic on the ZX Spectrum on which it was first developed, and was then ported to the Commodore 64 and Amstrad CPC.

Lords of Midnight had an innovative landscaping technique that allowed each of the 4,000 in-game locations to be seen from eight different viewpoints, providing as many as 32,000 different screenshots.

Seven Cities of Gold (1984, Electronic Arts)

It was for this game that today's common word "edutainment" was used for the very first time. Electronic Arts' founder Trip Hawkins, in fact, coined the word while presenting

Seven Cities of Gold, originally released for the Atari 8-bit, Apple II, and C64, put a lot of effort into recreating the original settings. Many details and historical references were included not only through good graphics, but also by using appropriate musical settings.

the game to the press to underscore its efforts to recreate an historical period and thereby serve as a history teaching tool, not just a fun game.

The gameplay, designed by Dan Bunten, started in 1492 where the player took the role of a Spanish conquistador embarking on the mission of exploring the New World[25] to retrieve as many treasures as possible for the Queen of Spain. To achieve this, he had to carefully plan where to build forts and missions and decide how to behave with the local populations—he could try to trade peacefully or to reach his objectives by being more aggressive. Interestingly, the variety of approaches available was also an effective tool for making players aware of their moral choices, adding a new layer of depth to the experience and achieving something that no other game had delivered before.

Despite clearly being a strategy game at its core, *Seven Cities of Gold* also featured original arcade sequences that made it a unique and groundbreaking product able to influence and inspire many other games and game designers.

Little Computer People (1985, Activision)

Created by David Crane and Sam Nelson, *Little Computer People* introduced a groundbreaking concept and delivered one of the most charming experiences ever on a variety of platforms, including the Apple II, Commodore 64, Amstrad CPC, ZX Spectrum, and, later, on 16-bit systems. The premise of the game was the discovery of a little man (and his dog) living inside the computer; the player's task was to follow them during their daily lives and help whenever needed. The player could watch the man in every room (except the bathroom) and, for example, could suggest to him

---

[25] Players could choose between the actual world and a randomly generated one.

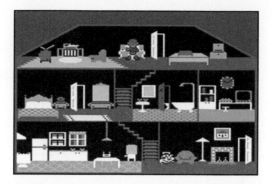

It's difficult to evaluate the heritage of this beautifully crafted game; it's likely that it is responsible for starting the life-simulation genre and it may even be somewhat responsible for the reality shows we see today on TV.

that he enjoy and practice several different activities like playing the piano or even playing computer games. Once in a while, he'd stop, sit at his typewriter, and write a letter to the player providing valuable feedback about the player's actions, explaining whether he was having a good life. His letters would let the player know whether he or she was perceived as a wise and responsible house owner or whether something needed to be improved. Graphics, animation, and sound effects were very cute and it didn't take long for many players to feel like the little man was really a part of their own family.

The Legend of Zelda (1986, Nintendo)

Another of Shigeru Miyamoto's everlasting successes, *The Legend of Zelda*[26] was a Nintendo exclusive for the NES released on February 21, 1986, and soon turned into one of the most beloved game franchises ever. Here, the player followed a cute, young elf named Link in a series of adventures across a vast fantasy land featuring lakes, forests, and dungeons with an intense action-based gameplay that included puzzle-solving and role-playing elements. The aims of the quest were to collect the scattered pieces of a magical artifact, the Triforce, that was needed to restore balance in the Universe, and then to save Princess Zelda.

The game was made unique by avoiding the common linear level-based structure typical of most console games and, instead, it granted complete freedom to the player to navigate the world. Link could also use many different items and meet a varied set of characters with whom the player could interact across his journey, allowing for several different gameplay styles and progress strategies. *The Legend of Zelda* was also notable for unlocking a "Second Quest" mode after the game was completed a

---

[26] The game was codesigned with Takashi Tezuka.

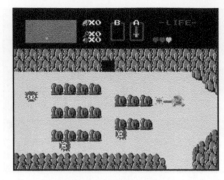

The original *Legend of Zelda* for the NES. Link's adventures started here.

first time, featuring not only stronger enemies but also new locations and different dungeons.

Metroid (1986, Nintendo)

Produced by Gunpei Yokoi and designed by Hiroji Kiyotake and Yoshio Sakamoto, *Metroid* was another of the extremely successful game franchises started in the eighties by Nintendo for its NES console and it was released in Japan during August 1986.[27] *Metroid* was a sci-fi adventure set on a hostile planet named Zebes with emphasis on cavern exploration and fighting against space pirates to rescue a number of stolen creatures, the Metroids, which could potentially be used to destroy entire worlds. The settings were made more interesting by the unconventional choice of the main character, a female bounty hunter named Samus Aran,[28] and by a set of specific game mechanics that were granted through different weapons and power-ups (for example, Samus could morph into a ball and move into otherwise inaccessible areas).

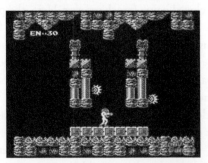

Exploring dangerous caves on planet Zebes.

---

[27] *Metroid* was released in North America in 1987 and in Europe only at the beginning of 1988.

[28] Characters and scenarios were conceived by Makoto Kanoh.

Unexpected twists were plenty, from discovering that the brave hero was actually a woman, to a frantic race back to safety once the player realized that defeating the final boss, Mother Brain, triggered a self destructing mechanism for the whole enemy lair.

Final Fantasy (1987, Square)

Created by Hironobu Sakaguchi and released in January 1987 on the NES, *Final Fantasy* marked the beginning of the longest running RPG series in the gaming industry. Interestingly, though, it wasn't actually created with the idea of making an everlasting franchise. Its name, in fact, showed the intent of creating a standalone game and the "final" one by Sakaguchi whose idea was to quit Square and go back to college to complete his university studies.[29]

Final Fantasy was a groundbreaking title in many respects, starting with its presentation. Even its cover art, in fact, took a completely different stance from all other NES games. While these usually showed simple, cartoonish, and blocky images, *Final Fantasy* opted for a more mysterious and fantastic approach and featured a town suspended in a crystal bowl together with the subtitle "Enter a whole new realm of challenge and adventure."

Original box artwork for the American release of *Final Fantasy*.

[29] It is commonly believed that Square was struggling financially and was near bankruptcy, so the "Final" in the title implied that it was possibly the last game before the company had to close down, which didn't happen thanks to the game's huge success. However, this appears to be just another myth and is refuted by Chris Kohler in his excellent book *Power Up* (p. 93) where he points out how most of Square's previous titles were actually successful from a commercial perspective and cites Sakaguchi's personal reasons as the only ones behind his choosing of the name (Chris Kohler, *Power Up*. Indianapolis, IN: BradyGames, 2004).

The world map and the battle screen. The player could choose four members from across six different classes, spanning warriors and mages, each with a different set of abilities and able to use only specific items and spells.

Notably, the game also began without a traditional splashscreen but started in a more cinematic way by using a scrolling text, clearly referencing movies like *Star Wars*. This little detail contributed significantly to adding a new, cinematic feeling to the whole experience. After the text scrolling, the player was able to start a new game by choosing a party of four characters instead of the usual single hero, and only then would an actual splashscreen appear.

Final Fantasy was set in a dark, oppressed world waiting for four Light Warriors— the player—to come forward and restore things to normalcy. Gameplay transpired through completely different screens: a world map to explore, towns in which to rest and to buy new equipment and spells, dungeons, and a turn-based battle screen in which to fight the numerous foes. Effectively mixing all of these different events and locations greatly contributed to delivering a grand new experience that was previously unheard of and made Japanese RPGs known internationally.

Maniac Mansion (1987, LucasFilm)

In the late eighties, text adventures faded away as graphics improved and became more integrated into the adventuring and exploring game mechanics. Additionally, building reliable text parsers was still a large task capable of monopolizing a huge chunk of available resources, so several companies started looking at alternative methods for delivering similarly engaging experiences. LucasFilm, thanks to SCUMM, a newly developed engine named after the first game it was used for (Script Creation Utility for *Maniac Mansion*), was one of the first companies to push adventures in a "point and click" direction where all available items, exits, and possible actions were identified on-screen without the user needing to type in all the respective names.

A screenshot right after entering the mansion.

Maniac Mansion, designed by Ron Gilbert and Gary Winnick, was the first in a long series of beautiful games that embraced this approach and saw the player in a mission to rescue Sandy, his missing girlfriend who was likely abducted to a mansion inhabited by a reclusive and mysterious family. At the beginning of the game, the player would arrange a small team by adding two more characters from a list of possible friends willing to help, each with his or her own personality and abilities. The player would venture into the mansion to solve a series of puzzles, mostly by combining objects in different ways, to ultimately rescue Sandy.

The new interface worked extremely well and, together with the quirkiness of the story, characters, graphics, and hilarious situations, it made *Maniac Mansion* a tremendous success that was ported to many different systems, starting from the Commodore 64, PC, and Apple II to 16-bit machines and the NES.

Part III

Sixteen-bit power, new generations, and
the rise of the PC

The Beginning of a New Era

The second half of the eighties saw big changes looming on the horizon of the gaming industry. Technology was advancing at an incredibly fast pace and new home computers started driving a wave of innovation thanks to more powerful and advanced 16-bit processors. In 1985, while the popularity of the arcades was slowly fading away in favor of home entertainment, both Atari and Commodore were ready to release their first ST and Amiga models, respectively.

Atari ST

At Atari, after the drastic restructuring approach put into practice by Jack Tramiel, new products started to be deployed very quickly. The focus, predictably, was on home computers: new 8-bit models—the XE series—were released while the game console business, which featured the 7800 and the restyled 2600 Jr., was relegated

The Atari ST was the first computer featuring a bit-mapped color GUI. It also had integrated MIDI ports, which made it the first choice for electronic musicians who could now control their instruments straight from the computer.

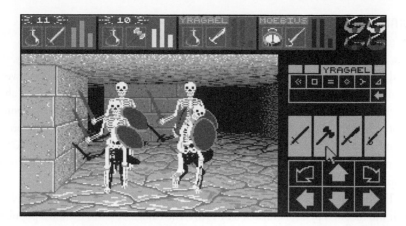

Dungeon Master (by FTL Games, 1987) was the first real-time 3D game with RPG elements and was developed on the Atari ST, where it became the best selling software of all time, in addition to being elected Adventure Game of the Year in the 1988 UK Software Industry Awards. It was then ported to the Amiga, Apple IIGS, DOS, and SNES.

to a supporting role to finance the computer R&D activity. While this made many "hard core" gamers of the time extremely unhappy, Jack's approach was, once again, valid from a business perspective. He made the company solvent, repaying Warner in just two and a half years, and brought the company public again in November 1986 after posting a profit of $45 million on sales of $258 million—an amazing feat considering the financial situation of the company after the crash. One of the main developments responsible for this impressive comeback was the ST line of home computers.

The first Atari ST, with 520 KB RAM and the Motorola 68000 CPU, was released in 1985 and it was the computer that Jack, together with his son Sam, was most proud of. The "ST" stood for "Sixteen/Thirty-two," referring to the 68000 16-bit external bus and 32-bit internals.

Different iterations with minor but significant improvements were released in the following years, such as adding more RAM, an integrated floppy drive, and so on. In 1989, a major upgrade took place in the form of the ST Enhanced (STE) model with improved multimedia and OS features, including a 4096-color palette (the original ST had only 512) and a graphics coprocessor (the Blitter) to handle on-screen manipulation of big chunks of data (representing big sprites, for example) more efficiently. The ST was especially successful in northern and central Europe where it also had a significant role in game development.

In 1992, a last upgrade was released in the form of the Falcon, a powerful machine with a 68030 CPU, but the computer was discontinued soon afterwards (in 1993) to allow Atari to focus on the upcoming Jaguar console instead.

Commodore Amiga

Once Jack Tramiel quit, Commodore was in dire need of a new hit and, luckily, they found it in the Amiga. The Amiga was planned from the ground up to be a powerful gaming machine and, indeed, its multimedia and graphical qualities were well ahead of their time thanks to a set of specific custom chips: Agnus, the central component responsible for accessing the chip's dedicated RAM; Denise, the main video processor; and Paula, the audio chip (later referenced all together under the name OCS, or Original Chip Set). The OCS endowed the machine with fast and powerful image manipulation and video editing abilities.

The first model, released in 1985 soon after the Atari ST launch, was the Amiga 1000, which was followed by the Amiga 500 in 1987. The Amiga 500 was the most popular of the series and, within the European region, it succeeded in replacing the Commodore 64 as the most popular home computer.

Several other Amiga models followed, featuring revisions and upgrades for the OCS, such as the Enhanced Chip Set (ECS) and Advanced Graphics Architecture (AGA). The last model, the Amiga 4000, sported a 32-bit Motorola 68040 CPU (or, in a different configuration to reduce costs, a 68EC030) and was released in 1992.

Built around the Motorola 68000 CPU and thanks to the addition of specific customized chips, Amiga computers soon became the favorite tool for video editing and graphic manipulation purposes. Many graphical software packages still common nowadays, like Blender and LightWave 3D, were first released on this platform.

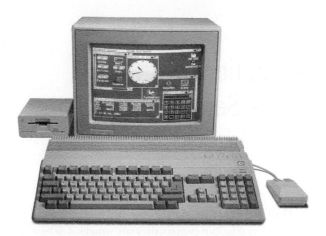

The Amiga 500. With 512 KB RAM, it was the entry machine in the Amiga series. It also became the most popular one and the gaming machine of choice for many European teenagers during the late eighties and early nineties.

Overall, games were obviously what made the Amiga so attractive to many young people, but the Amiga was also widely used by professionals thanks not only to its graphical prowess but also to a very advanced operating system, the AmigaOS, which was one of the very first commercial ones to allow preemptive multitasking[1] and to combine both a friendly GUI and a command line interface.

Shadow of the Beast, a side-scroller action/adventure game developed by Reflections Interactive and published by Psygnosis in 1989, pushed home gaming to new heights. Extremely colorful environments, detailed sprites, 12 levels of parallax scrolling, and atmospheric music featuring high quality samples made a truly unique experience that was later ported to many other home computers and gaming consoles.

---

[1] Preemptive multitasking is a method that allows a CPU to divide its processing time regularly across several processes to allow the user to run multiple applications at once.

New Generations with
Some of the Same Old Problems
• •

During the second half of the eighties, video games had firmly regained their spot in the hearts of kids and teenagers alike, but even so, they still struggled to be widely accepted by a large part of society. Many people, in fact, still saw video games as a potential "danger" that was capable of negatively affecting the impressionable minds of the youth.

As the most well-known game developer of the time, Nintendo, despite its continuous efforts to appear "family friendly" from the very beginning of the NES launch, became the main target of different groups for many different reasons. Jewish associations harshly criticized Nintendo for designing a dungeon in *The Legend of Zelda* in the shape of a swastika.[2] Parents flooded the company with angry phone calls following the release of *Castlevania II: Simon's Quest* and its review in the official Nintendo magazine *Nintendo Power* because the artwork, featuring the main character holding a severed Dracula's head, gave their kids nightmares. In general, like in the early eighties, video games were an easy target to blame for making kids lazy or more aggressive. Groups such as Families for Peace started demonstrating in front of Nintendo of America headquarters to protest the use of guns in games. Even academic professors began analyzing the social implications of the video game phenomena, with some concluding that video games were very harmful because they actually instigated violence and racism.[3]

Fortunately, this strong negative perception by certain parts of society was not enough to trigger another collapse spanning the whole industry. Most of the other elements that we discussed as causes of the 1983 crash were now absent as the industry had greatly matured. Besides, the technological advances provided by new 16-bit CPUs and their first forays into home computers showed that the time for a new generation of dedicated gaming machines was also approaching. This time, video games were here to stay.

---

[2] A symbol in the shape of a swastika is actually common in Buddhism and this might have been the actual reference for the dungeon layout.

[3] Eugene F. Provenzo. *Video Kids: Making Sense of Nintendo*. Cambridge, MA: Harvard University Press, 1991. For example, the book cites the game Teenage Mutant Ninja Turtles for instigating racism towards Asian people because the bad guys were Japanese ninjas.

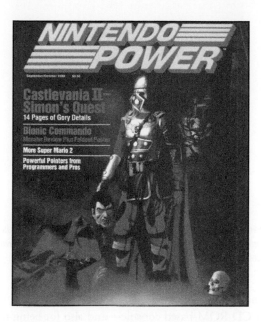

The infamous cover of Nintendo Power #2 (September/October 1988), featuring *Castlevania II: Simon's Quest* for the NES that disturbed the peaceful sleep of many kids, triggering a flood of angry phone calls to Nintendo by upset parents.

PC Engine/TurboGrafx-16

The first company to release a new, more powerful console to rival the NES was NEC with the PC Engine. This console was first released in Japan for the 1987 holiday season and became known as the TurboGrafx-16 in the United States where it was released in August 1989.[4]

Even though the PC Engine was still an 8-bit machine at its core, it had a significant amount of horsepower thanks to an original three chip architecture designed by Hudson Soft that, besides a customized 8-bit CPU,[5] also included two 16-bit GPUs able to handle many sprites on screen and display hundreds of different colors simultaneously from a palette of 512.[6]

---

[4] The PC Engine was never officially released in Europe even though it was available as a parallel import through some major retailers in France and other countries.

[5] This was the HuC6280, which added more instructions and a programmable sound generator, among other features, to the 65SC02 processor.

[6] Up to 241 colors were available for sprites while another lot of 241 could have been selected for backgrounds, bringing the total to a staggering 482.

The original Japanese version of the PC Engine. Games were released in small cards and the console was very popular in Japan where it even outsold the NES. Several different iterations were released between 1987 and 1994 and, overall, about 10 million units were sold worldwide.

The PC Engine was also notable for the addition of an optional CD module—making it the first CD-ROM-based console—and also for being the smallest home console ever, measuring only 14 cm × 14 cm × 3.8 cm (5.5" × 5.5" × 1.5").

Regarding video games, NEC's console excelled in porting arcade shooters but lacked top-notch original titles and memorable characters, with the possible exception of Bonk. Most likely it was this weakness, coupled with some unlucky marketing choices and, most importantly, a slow localization process for making the successful Japanese games sellable in other markets, that severely limited the appeal of its overall catalogue and prevented the system from gaining a larger following worldwide.

Bonk's Adventure, released in 1990, made the cute bald caveman Bonk one of the most popular characters born on the PC Engine. The game was also ported on the Amiga (as B.C. Kid) and then even on the rival NES.

Mega Drive/Genesis

After gaining international exposure in the home console space with the Master System, Sega was ready to step up to the competition with a new, much more powerful unit based on the 68000 processor. The Mega Drive, renamed Genesis in the United States, debuted in Japan in time for the 1988 holiday season. Even though the reception in Japan wasn't enthusiastic due to the strong competition from the PC Engine, Sega was hopeful that its machine would be a hit in Europe and even in the North American market, possibly breaking into Nintendo's stronghold.

To achieve its ambitious objectives, Sega's strategy was articulated across different points, spanning all aspects of marketing and new ways to attract audiences as well as third-party developers. First and foremost, there was the need to emphasize the technical superiority of the Genesis against the older NES. The game chosen to be bundled with the console was Sega's port of its own arcade title *Altered Beast*. This game, while not a memorable experience in terms of gameplay, showed that the system could handle faithful arcade renditions with colorful graphics and giant, detailed sprites in contrast to the usually tiny and less defined graphics of the 8-bit NES. The NES was also targeted directly in Sega's advertising campaign through a series of bold ads built around the "Genesis does what Nintendon't" slogan to make the new system look "cooler" in the eyes of a young crowd (see the figure on the top of page 124).

The Mega Drive, rebranded Genesis in the United States where it debuted, like the PC Engine, during August 1989. The Genesis retailed at a price of $189 and games could display up to 64 colors on-screen from a palette of 512 while sound was handled by a dedicated Zilog Z-80 processor, like in many arcade machines of the time.

One of the famous ads designed for the aggressive marketing campaign put on by Sega to lure away Nintendo's user base. This ad features Michael Jackson's Moonwalker game (1990).

To make the system attractive to old and new players alike, Sega's strategy was two-fold. First, the Genesis was retro-compatible with the Master System, a feature that was especially appreciated in Europe where Sega's 8-bit console was more popular. Second, like Electronic Arts did with its pioneering basketball game *One on One: Dr. J vs. Larry Bird*, Sega tied new games to famous personalities to encourage instant awareness and excitement about the titles. *Joe Montana's Football*, *Pat Riley's Basketball*, *Arnold Palmer's Golf*, and even *Michael Jackson's Moonwalker* were all quickly added to the catalogue to appeal to fans worldwide.

Another noteworthy aspect of Sega's policies was the effort in getting relevant third-party support for the console. Nintendo still had very strict policies for its developers and Sega offered much better deals—in addition to better royalties, companies could publish as many games as they wanted and they could even "greenlight" games themselves.[7] Electronic Arts was one of the first developers to release games for the Genesis and other companies soon followed, providing the system with a good and varied catalogue. Most importantly, though, the real breakthrough for the Genesis happened once they featured an iconic character, Sonic the Hedgehog, who was able to rival even Super Mario in popularity.

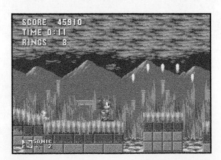

A screenshot from the original *Sonic the Hedgehog*, programmed by Yuji Naka with the main character designed by Naoto Oshima. The game was released in 1991. Running at high speed across colorful levels added new excitement to side-scrolling action games.

---

[7] At that time, Nintendo still limited each company to publish no more than five games per year and all games had to be approved beforehand.

Lastly, to keep the offer fresh and lengthen the system lifespan, Sega also offered a very valuable add-on, first released in Japan in 1991: the Mega-CD, which provided access to CD-based games as well as allowed users to play music CDs.

All of these concerted efforts succeeded in putting the Mega Drive on the international map and fueled the sales of about 30 million units worldwide. At least half were bought in the North American market, bringing Sega to own a 55% share of all 16-bit hardware sales during 1994 in North America.[8]

Super Nintendo Entertainment System

The NES was definitely starting to show its age compared to the new competitors, but Nintendo, relying on its leadership position in the North American market with a NES user base of about 20 million and 1989 sales topping $2.3 billion, rested on its laurels for a while before realizing that the Genesis was becoming a serious threat.

The Super Nintendo Entertainment System (SNES), known as Super Famicom in Japan, was designed by Masayuki Uemura (who was also responsible for the hardware design of the NES) and went on sale in Japan on November 21, 1990, at about $210. Despite a very limited catalogue of titles available at launch, including only *Super Mario World* (see the figure on the top of page 126) and *F-Zero*, the success was so huge[9] that it seriously disrupted everyday life and activities. In the end, the resulting chaos in the middle of the working week had such an impact that the Japanese government had to officially ask game companies to plan for important launches on weekends in the future.

The SNES (here in the North American version) was built around a Ricoh 5A22 CPU, based on a 16-bit 65C816 core, and had 64 KB of video RAM. Colors could be chosen from a palette of 32,768, and up to 128 sprites and four layers of background could be displayed at once. Interestingly, audio was handled by the 8-bit Sony SPC700 chip that, designed by Ken Kutaragi, represented Sony's first foray into the video game arena.

---

[8] Jane Greenstein. "Game makers dispute who is market leader." *Video Business* (January 15, 1995).

[9] The first shipment of 300,000 units sold out in just a few hours.

Super Mario World was one of only two titles available at launch in Japan and it was bundled with the American and European consoles, launched in August 1991 and April 1992, respectively.

One of the peculiar aspects of the SNES was its way of handling the possibility of future enhancements through add-on chips that were incorporated into the game cartridges themselves. This was a clever way of updating and expanding the technical capabilities of the console, granting it a longer lifespan and the ability to compete with more modern systems released by its competitors. On the other hand, though, it also meant higher cartridge manufacturing costs.

Math and digital signal processing (DSP) coprocessors were developed by Nintendo as well as by third parties like Capcom, but the most important and well-known chip was the Super-FX. It was developed by London-based Argonaut Games and added a RISC-based CPU to properly handle 3D graphics and special 2D effects.

Nintendo also explored online services for the first time. In Japan, the Satellaview, a modem able to connect to a satellite radio station, was released in 1995 allowing

The space shooter *Star Fox*, codeveloped by Nintendo and Argonaut Games in 1993, was the first game to show what the Super-FX could do to render 3D polygon-based graphics.

players to download new games and take part in online tournaments.[10] In the United States, Nintendo instead partnered with XBAND, an online gaming network that, through a standard dial-up modem connection and a monthly fee starting at $4.95, allowed gamers to play with each other across the country. The service, which was also used by Sega for the Genesis, started towards the end of 1994 but never succeeded in becoming very popular and was ultimately discontinued in 1997.

Despite its late start, the SNES succeeded in becoming the best-selling console of the 16-bit era with 49.1 million units sold worldwide during its long lifespan.[11] Despite this success, Sega, thanks to its aggressive and varied strategies, still challenged Nintendo and the whole industry in other ways. Games like *Mortal Kombat*, where players could compete in very gory fights featuring plenty of blood, dismembering, and decapitations, were still heavily censored by Nintendo with the result that the more "open" attitude by Sega made the Genesis port of the game outsell the SNES by a large margin. Such extremely violent gameplay also prompted the formation of new official bodies, like the Entertainment Software Rating Board (ESRB), to properly rate games by relating their content to suitable age groups. This allowed Nintendo to relax its policies a bit and, indeed, the SNES version of *Mortal Kombat II*, which kept all the gory details, actually outsold versions on any other system.

Neo-Geo

The Neo-Geo, released in 1990 by the Japanese company SNK, was a unique system used both as an arcade machine and as a home console due to its small size and cartridge-based approach. It was usually known as the Multi Video System (MVS) and the Advance Entertainment System (AES) when used in arcades or homes, respectively.

The Neo-Geo console. It was a dual processor machine, with a 16-bit 68000 CPU plus an 8-bit Zilog Z-80 coprocessor as well as custom video and audio chipsets. The dual CPU architecture gave the idea to some cunning marketing executive to present the console as a "24-bit system" (i.e., 16 plus 8 bits).

---

[10] The service was discontinued on June 30, 2000.

[11] The SNES was officially discontinued in 1999 and 2003 in North America and Japan, respectively.

A screenshot from *The King of Fighters '94,* the first in the long-lasting and successful series.

While the Neo-Geo was a very smart and economical choice for arcade use since up to six different titles could be fit into a single cabinet, the price was very steep for those who wanted to bring the system home as a gaming console: $650. And if that wasn't enough, each cartridge had a price tag typically between $200 and $300. Obviously, this made the system not really viable for the home market but made it a coveted item for a niche market of hardcore enthusiasts and collectors.

The Neo-Geo was able to handle colorful graphics (up to 4,096 colors) and big sprites. Several fighting game franchises like *The King of Fighters* and *Samurai Showdown,* and scrolling action games like *Metal Slug,* were originally developed for it. Overall, 154 games were released, with the last official title, *Samurai Showdown V Special,* released in 2004.

3DO Interactive Multiplayer

The 3DO Company[12] was founded in 1991 by Trip Hawkins, one of Electronic Arts cofounders, together with key industry players such as LG, Matsushita, AT&T, Time Warner, and Electronic Arts itself, with the idea of bringing to market a new CD-based gaming console that, by following a strict set of specifications, could be manufactured by several partners. The 3DO Interactive Multiplayer was released with a lot of hype in 1993 (see Figure 144). However, the very steep launch price of $699 prevented it from building a user base wide enough to attract game developers despite the generous royalty program offered by the company and the advanced technical capabilities of the system, which was built around a 32-bit ARM60 CPU with two custom video chipsets and a math coprocessor.

---

[12] The original name was SMSG Inc.

The 3DO system was manufactured by the likes of Panasonic, Sanyo, and Goldstar thanks to a standard-ized set of specifications, as was previously done for computers such as the MSX models. Interestingly, it had only one controller port but up to eight gamepads could have been plugged into each other in a daisy chain fashion.

The 3DO tried to be a complete entertainment system and focal point of the living room where users could play audio and video CDs in addition to games. Unfortunately, its gaming catalogue was, for the most part, uninteresting and lacked appealing exclusive titles. Even though more than 200 titles were released, CD-based games were at their dawn and developers were still in the process of figuring out the new and unique possibilities offered by the medium. In the end, many of the result-ing games were sort of "interactive movies" with low-quality full motion videos and very little interactivity—basically, players could only develop the storyline by select-ing one event from among a few predefined branching possibilities, but this wasn't enough to keep them interested and the new genre failed to attract a proper audience. At this time, in fact, gamers seemed not really keen on such an experience that, al-though original, was neither as relaxing as watching a good movie nor as engaging as playing a good game.[13] Ultimately, the system was discontinued in 1996 after having sold only about two million units worldwide.

---

[13] The Sega-CD had the same problem too but, luckily, the Mega Drive/Genesis standard catalogue of games was good enough to keep the system alive.

1991: Sony and Nintendo?

• • • • • • • • • • • • • • • • • •

After having started a fruitful cooperation with Nintendo in 1988 to develop the audio chip for the SNES, Sony became more and more interested in the video game industry and keen to explore new possibilities in the market.

As an extension of the previous agreement, Sony, still under the guidance of Ken Kutaragi, started developing a special CD add-on device, named Super Disc, for the SNES. This device would have allowed the system to play both cartridge titles and the upcoming breed of bigger CD-based games, with Sony retaining the rights for the latter. At the same time, the tech giant also started planning for its own CD-based and SNES-compatible console, code-named Play Station. At the June 1991 CES in Chicago, the new projects were finally unveiled to the public.

Sony's growing interest in the video game market and its aggressive new plans, though, started to worry Nintendo. Realizing that they were losing control of the upcoming CD-ROM market in favor of their new "partner," Nintendo decided to cancel the agreement with Sony right after the CES announcement and, instead,

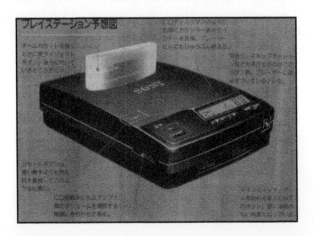

A Play Station prototype as shown in a Japanese magazine. Note the cartridge slot on top to play SNES games. Like the 3DO and the Philips CD-i, the Play Station was meant from the very beginning to play not only games but also movies and other multimedia applications.

A SNES mounting the CD add-on prototype. The project was ultimately cancelled because Nintendo later decided to focus its energies on a completely new system, the Nintendo 64, instead of revamping the "old" SNES.

signed a more advantageous deal with Philips[14] for a similar SNES add-on. In this arrangement, Nintendo would retain all the rights from CD-based games running on their console.

This move, by completely removing Sony from the SNES scene, also seemed to kick out the tech giant from the whole gaming world for good. But Mr. Kutaragi was a firm believer in the upcoming possibilities for Sony in the video game and home entertainment markets. After struggling to keep the interest alive in spite of the disillusionment of several Sony executives, he was allowed to work on a completely new and SNES-independent system that was destined to change the gaming landscape for many years to come: the PlayStation.

---

[14] At the time, Philips was also working on a CD-based product named CD-i that was released in October 1991 with a $1,000 price tag. The system, able to play a variety of disc formats besides games, sold less than one million units worldwide and didn't have any meaningful impact on the gaming industry.

The PC Becomes Gaming Mature

As the gaming industry kept expanding and becoming increasingly popular thanks to new dedicated consoles and home computers, more and more people found themselves needing different systems for play and for work. In fact, while computers like the Commodore Amiga and Atari ST were very popular choices at home and for specific jobs like video or music editing, the IBM PC and compatibles were by far the most common option for general business use; unfortunately, they were not able to deliver any meaningful entertainment value due to a severe lack of multimedia capabilities.

It's no wonder that attempts to bring together the two worlds were soon proposed by different manufacturers, hoping to make their products valuable to anybody needing something for both serious working applications as well as for some recreational time. For example, expansion modules featuring an Intel 8088 CPU to provide the performance of an XT series PC running MS-DOS were developed for the Amiga in the late eighties and even a two-in-one system produced by IBM for Sega named TeraDrive was released in Japan in 1991.

The TeraDrive was essentially a Mega Drive built together with a PC AT Series featuring an Intel 286 CPU where the user had the ability to switch easily between the two machines at start up. It was never released outside of Japan but it had a successor, the Mega PC, manufactured by Amstrad and released in 1993 in Europe and Australia, which coupled the Mega Drive with an Intel 386-based PC.

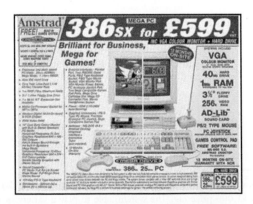

A British ad for the Amstrad/Sega Mega PC, a 386sx-based IBM PC compatible that integrated a Mega Drive to easily alternate work and play.

Unfortunately, all of these hybrids had the serious issue of trying to match two very fast moving but independent industries and the PC configurations that were provided were already old by the time the systems were launched. Ultimately, none of them succeeded in impressing the general public. The PC industry, on the other hand, finally understood the huge market opportunities that were available by approaching the games industry, and the PC world started moving even faster while finally covering the areas where it had been left behind. For example, in 1987, Creative Technologies, a company founded in Singapore in 1981, started releasing sound cards that enabled PCs to go beyond the extremely simple sounds and beeps that were common across workstations in the eighties. The first SoundBlaster card was released in 1989 and the first stereo models were available by 1992. At about the same time, other companies took care of expanding the graphical prowess of personal computers.

Canadian ATI Technologies, founded in 1985 under the name Array Technologies Incorporated, soon started developing integrated graphic cards for both IBM and Commodore. In May 1991, it released the Mach8, their first card able to process graphics without the need for the computer's own CPU. Improved versions soon followed. In 1994, the Mach64 debuted and was then expanded into the 3D Rage series, which could provide enough power to handle 3D graphics effectively.

ATI wasn't the only company to rise quickly in the graphics segment, though, and companies such as S3, Matrox, and Nvidia all rapidly gained importance. In particular, Nvidia, founded in California in 1993, was ready to release its first product by 1995—the NV1. It was sold as the Diamond Edge 3D graphics card and also featured an integrated sound card to rival Creative's SoundBlaster. While the NV1 wasn't as successful as other models, like the ATI Rage or the S3 ViRGE, it allowed Nvidia to get a solid foothold in the market and start a line of GPUs[15] that became increasingly popular year after year.

At last, more power and possibilities were finally available to computers that were originally conceived as working machines and, by the early to mid-nineties, IBM PCs were finally able to handle multimedia applications properly including, obviously, games.

It was within this new exciting context that a group of friends, including programmers John Carmack and John Romero, designer Tom Hall and artist Adrian Carmack, started developing software and simple games for *SoftDisk*, a floppy disk-based monthly magazine. At the same time, they also began working on their own projects to make something much more advanced and unique.

John Carmack in particular succeeded in developing a 2D game engine featuring a very smooth scrolling action that was used to develop an unofficial PC port of *Super Mario 3*. The demo was showcased to Nintendo but the big company was not

---

[15] Graphics Processing Unit, a specialized microprocessor built for the purpose of offloading the main CPU from graphics computations to vastly accelerate rendering.

interested in bringing Mario to the PC and the game code was then reused to develop a completely new and original game, *Commander Keen*. Released in December 1990, *Commander Keen* quickly became a hit in the burgeoning shareware PC market and, once the group realized the quality of their programming skills and the possibilities ahead of them, they left *SoftDisk* to start their own company, ID Software, which was officially founded on February 1, 1991.

Experimenting with the new PC hardware capabilities and 3D graphics became a priority at ID Software and the first PC 3D game, *Hovertank 3D*, was released in April 1991.

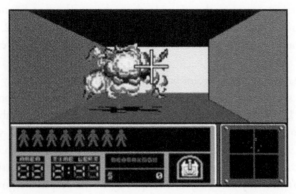

Hovertank 3D, the first 3D game developed by the newly founded ID Software in 1991. The 3D walls had no texture yet but such fast, 3D gameplay action was already an amazing step forward from anything previously seen on a PC screen.

Hovertank was soon followed by a more refined project, *Catacomb 3D*, released in November 1991 and then, in early May 1992, *Wolfenstein 3D* was ready. The experience gained from the two previous games allowed for the crafting of a frenetic first-person experience filled with hectic and non-stop shooting action that changed the face of PC gaming forever.

Wolfenstein 3D featured an Allied spy, named B.J. Blazkowicz, trapped in a castle serving as a Nazi base. Escaping alive by killing as many SS soldiers as possible was the only aim, providing hours of exciting and heart-stopping action.

By the early nineties, with new and more powerful multimedia hardware and amazing new games that could rival those on any other system, the PC was finally a working tool and quickly became a viable entertainment platform. Once this was acknowledged, it started spreading to homes where it slowly began to take on a central role in the lives of many people.

Games That Pushed Boundaries III

· ·

With more computational power available, delivering more cinematic and realistic gaming experiences was now possible and a new breed of complex, engaging, and immersive titles emerged on all available platforms.

Sid Meier's Pirates! (1987, MicroProse)

By expanding and refining the formula of mixing strategy and action in a real, exciting historical setting, *Sid Meier's Pirates!* was the groundbreaking title that firmly annointed Sid Meier as one of the leading figures on the global game design scene. Presented as the "world's first swashbuckling simulation," the game started by letting the player choose a particular historical period (ranging from the late 16th to mid-18th centuries), a nationality (English, French, Dutch, or Spanish) and a special ability (e.g., fencing, navigation, etc.). The gameplay that followed was an exciting mix of strategy and action, with sword duels, naval battles, and interaction possibilities with several NPCs. The latter followed a typical adventure-style approach by giving simple dialogue/action options but included also the uncommon feature of practicing seductive skills with the beautiful daughters of local governors.

A duel taking place on an Atari ST.

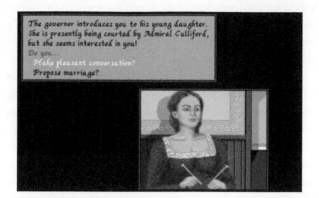

An Amiga screenshot of the governor's beautiful daughter.

First released on the Commodore 64, Apple II, and Amstrad CPC in 1987, the game soon went on to exploit the 16-bit multimedia capabilities of the Atari ST in 1989 and the Amiga in 1990 and was then ported to many other systems and consoles,[16] singlehandedly making pirate characters "cool" in the gaming world.

Captain Blood (1988, ERE Informatique)

"Welcome to the age of the bio game." With these enigmatic words, different advertisements introduced *Captain Blood,* in which the NPCs in the game were able to

Amiga screenshot of an attempt to get some meaningful information by talking to an alien. All communication had to be done by expressing ideas through a set of icons selected by using the robotic arm.

---

[16] Interestingly, *Pirates!* is somewhat of an oddity among successful games since it is one of the very few that had plenty of remakes instead of sequels over the years.

carry on with their lives independent of the player's actions. In this very original sci-fi adventure game, designed by Didier Buchon and Philippe Ulrich and published by Infogrames and Mindscape on a variety of home computers, an unlucky programmer was cloned and trapped in his own game and needed to quickly find and kill all of his clones to avoid being mutated into a robot forever. In particular, there were five clones hidden somewhere in the systems of a huge galaxy featuring as many as 32,768 planets that the player needed to explore while searching for clues. During the game, the player met many different alien creatures. Some were friendly, others more aggressive and, interestingly, the only way to communicate with them was through a set of universal icons that allowed the player to communicate regardless of the alien language spoken in a specific world.

Besides the unique icon-driven communication gameplay, the game is also worth remembering for its stunning flying sequence (one of the first of its kind to use fractal techniques) and for the impressive music by Jean Michel Jarre.

Snatcher (1988, Konami)

Created by Hideo Kojima for Konami and released first on MSX computers in 1988, *Snatcher* was ported to the TurboGrafx and Sega consoles in CD format, in 1992 and 1994 respectively, where it was hailed as one of the top and most engrossing games to date. Loosely reminiscent of sci-fi movies like *Blade Runner*, *Snatcher* was an adventure game set in Japan during a dark future where mankind was under attack by mysterious creatures with the ability to kill people and seamlessly merge into society by assuming their victims' identities. Within this nightmarish setting, the player took the role of a police officer trying to shed some light on the mystery and to expose any "snatcher" (i.e., a creature in human form).

A Sega CD screenshot depicting one of the many environments the player would explore and search in detail. In 1988, people already knew that floppy disks were doomed and CDs were the way to go!

The game was a masterpiece of storytelling where conversing with other characters was a key element to advance the plot while enabling the game to effectively alternate scary, comic, and even sensual moments. With effective manga-style graphics, proper voice acting, and plenty of locations and objects with which to interact, *Snatcher* showed what CD-based games could achieve at a time when too many developers were only trying to produce interactive movies with little replay value and appeal.

Prince of Persia (1989, Broderbund)

Created by Jordan Mechner and released first on the Apple II, *Prince of Persia* started an extremely successful gaming franchise that spawned sequels and ports on almost every other computer and system released ever since. The reasons for this lasting success were found in the merging of novel ways to experiment with technology together with a classic tale of love and courage. In particular, Mechner was able to obtain very smooth animations thanks to "rotoscoping"[17] short movie clips of his younger brother taken while running and jumping. These served as the foundation for developing a very believable world made up of dungeons, secret passages, and halls, where the characters could move in an engaging 2D platforming action.

Interestingly, the player in the game had an infinite number of lives but only one hour of actual time to save his beloved from marrying the evil vizier Jaffar, who concealed her in the highest tower of his castle. This original twist plus a mix of combat, running, and environmental puzzles requiring both strategic thinking and fast action, made for a very engaging and groundbreaking gaming experience that is still able to fascinate modern players.

A swordfight from the original *Prince of Persia* on the Apple II.

---

[17] An animation technique in which animators trace over live-action film movement, frame by frame.

Kick Off (1989, Anco)

With football (or soccer in America) being one of the most popular sports in the world, it's no wonder that many games dedicated to it were produced for any system ever released. Most of them tended to share a similar, simple gameplay where the ball was "glued" to the player who touched it, making it easy to control the action and move around the field until challenged by another player.

The first game that changed this approach and defined a more complex and difficult-to-master gameplay was *Kick Off*, designed and programmed by Dino Dini. Here, players could only "touch" the ball and had to keep running to follow it closely, making for much faster and challenging action. Moreover, a more realistic feeling was enhanced throughout the game by giving four different attributes to each player (Pace, Stamina, Accuracy, and Aggression) and by offering a set of 12 different referees with unique and moody personalities who could at times overlook bad tackles while mercilessly showing yellow and red cards to players on other occasions. In *Kick Off*, like in a real life, every new match was always unpredictable.

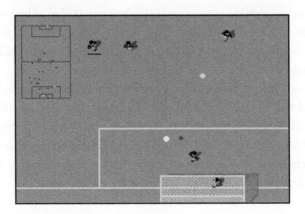

Kick Off, here on the Amiga, was also noteworthy for perfecting the top-down camera view that was first introduced in Championship Soccer for the Atari 2600 in 1980 but, this time, with much more realistic action, physics, and proper visuals.

SimCity (1989, Maxis/Infogrames)

SimCity was one of those rare games that successfully started a completely new genre and granted its creator, Will Wright, long-lasting fame.

The game concept was, in fact, so original that several game publishers at first rejected the project due to its uncommon settings. Many people didn't even consider it

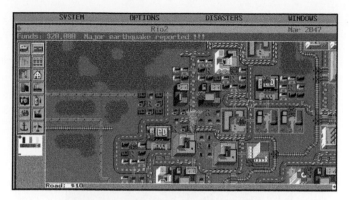

Building a unique city on a MS-DOS-based PC.

a "game" due to the fact that there was no real victory condition and the action could continue indefinitely.[18] The game is as simple in theory as it is difficult and fascinating in practice—the player is the mayor of a new municipality with the responsibility of building and maintaining a place where his or her citizens can have happy and fulfilling lives. In the process, the mayor has to plan for housing, streets, factories, etc., while also balancing pollution and traffic jams. Managing taxes properly was also a fundamental aspect of improving the quality of the public services while still keeping the citizens happy. To make things more unpredictable and exciting, floods, earthquakes, and other natural calamities were also possible, and this required good advance planning for storing enough resources to be used in times of need.

SimCity was so successful that many versions were developed for several computers, both 8- and 16-bits, in 1989 and 1990. In 1991, it was ported to the SNES and went on to define the whole sim genre that became so popular throughout the nineties and beyond.

Populous (1989, Bullfrog/EA)

While *SimCity* tasked the player with the role of mayor, *Populous* wasn't afraid to be much more ambitious and gave him or her the role of God.

Designed and coprogrammed by Peter Molyneux, the player had to lead his or her people in conquering the world and defeating the followers of the rival deity. The striking originality of the game lay not only in the concept itself but also in how the mechanics of indirectly controlling the followers were implemented. For instance, the player could flatten the land to enable the followers to gather resources, build

---

[18] To address this point, eight predefined time-limited scenarios with specific challenges and targets were added.

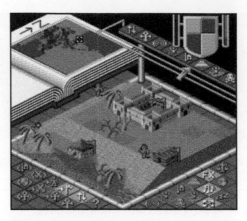

Populous was an RTS pioneer driven by a cleverly designed set of icons offering plenty of ways to interact with the men onscreen. Here is a screenshot from the SNES version.

cities, and become stronger before they were finally ready for a face-to-face battle with the enemy.

Released first on the Amiga, Atari ST, and MS-DOS in 1989 and then ported to consoles such as the SNES, Mega Drive, Master System, and TurboGrafx-16, *Populous* soon received rave reviews by the specialized press and became a classic in the emerging RTS genre.

Lost Patrol (1990, Shadow Development/Ocean)

A unique game among military and combat simulations, *Lost Patrol*, designed by Ian Harling, offered a different perspective on war from any other game released before or since.

While most productions, whether turn- and strategy-based simulations or fast-paced action shooters, tried to excite players to conquer new areas and kill enemies, *Lost Patrol* tried to show the real and ugly side of war through a very difficult and painful mission in which glory was unattainable. The game was set in the Vietnam War where the player took the lead of a squad of marines whose helicopter had been shot down in the jungle and whose only hope was to reach the nearest US military base on foot. Most of the game was played on a map where moving decisions were followed by an original war video sequence, showing the soldiers marching ahead, and a status report informing of any accidents/events that might have occurred in the meantime. Action sequences, like hand-to-hand combat with a lone Vietcong or a simple first-person shootout near a village, were possible and heightened the sense of risk and constant fear of what could lie ahead. Notably, even after "winning"

Lost Patrol on the Amiga. Atmospheric background music also helped in defining an extremely sorrowful mood; the game sought to make the player feel how weary and frustrated the wounded soldiers were as they dragged themselves through the Vietnamese jungle, where every step could mean death.

the game and saving the soldiers, the game ends in a very sober and even sad way, showing that there is no glory in war but only pain and destruction.

Civilization (1991, MicroProse)

Civilization was another masterpiece by Sid Meier and rapidly became his most successful game and most recognizable franchise. Indeed, *Civilization*'s massive scale and ambitious aims were unheard of before—to start your own nation and make it prosper from the Stone Age until the 21st century.

To succeed, players had to divide their strategies into several parts: build new cities, develop an army (both for offensive and defensive purposes), trade with neighboring countries, and invest in scientific research, all while maintaining a delicate balance in internal politics so their citizens felt satisfied and kept producing the resources necessary for further expansion.

In *Civilization*, anyone could have a chance to rule the world across the whole of human history and even meet historical figures face to face. Here is a screenshot from the original DOS version.

Civilization was first released on MS-DOS PCs (with programming done by Sid himself) and later ported to the Amiga, Atari ST, Apple Macintosh, and the SNES, always with great success.

Another World (1991, Delphine/U.S.Gold)

Also known as *Out of This World*, this game represented a breakthrough in storytelling for action/adventure games where a cinematic approach allowed a more streamlined experience and beautifully animated cut scenes effortlessly introduced the player into the virtual world. The player was a young and bold physics professor who found himself in an alternate world after he was struck by lightning during an experiment. Now it's up to the player to find a way to escape and, hopefully, go back home.

Plenty of environmental- and physics-based puzzles were present and the game was also made more challenging, and movie-like, by the absence of any user interface or dialogue screen whatsoever, making the player effectively feel helpless in an unknown, mysterious, and hostile world.

An Amiga screenshot of the first playable screen in the game where the professor had to escape before the tentacles of a monster caught him. Meanwhile, a mysterious lion-like beast watched from a distance.

Lemmings (1991, DMA Design/Psygnosis)

Designed by David Jones and first released for the Amiga and Atari ST computers in 1991, *Lemmings* was such a striking success that versions for many other systems and consoles, including the Sega Master System and Genesis; Nintendo NES, SNES, and Game Boy; and 3DO soon followed.[19]

---

[19] Versions for 28 different systems were actually developed.

Escaping a hellish environment on the SNES.

As the name suggests, the game was based around lemmings, a particular species of rodent believed to have suicidal tendencies, and the objective was to save as many as possible by herding them through 120 different and tricky levels. Each lemming could be given a specific task, such as climbing, digging, or floating. These tasks had to be combined to solve the different environmental puzzles in each level and over- come any obstacle, like drops, barriers, rivers, floating lava, and other lethal hazards, to reach the exit safely. The level design of the game was also impressive, smoothly advancing the player from simple tutorial-like levels to very complex and nightmar- ish challenges.

Street Fighter II (1991, Capcom)

From the early days of fighting games, two main subgenres developed. One was a more realistic type, pioneered by the likes of *Karate Champ*, which tried to mimic real tournament mechanics with a point-based scoring system. The other took a more fantastic approach with fighters able to perform amazing feats using different styles and weapons, as in *Yie Ar Kung Fu* by Konami (1985). In the latter, victory was not determined by "points" but by simply depleting the opponent's life bar with as many hits as needed. The more fantastic genre was the one to gain the biggest interest and popularity as soon as Capcom released the first *Street Fighter* game in 1987. This was then perfected and made even more impressive in 1991 with the arcade release of *Street Fighter II*, defining once and for all a benchmark against which any fighting game had to be compared ever since.

In *Street Fighter II,* players had a chance to fight against a multitude of differ- ent characters, each with a unique background, personality, and fighting style. Many

Street Fighter II as ported on the SNES. Here, Guile's Flash Kick move sends Ken far away.

different moves were available and could be combined in a variety of ways to render devastating combos. These required considerable skill to be mastered and used effectively, and added a layer of strategy and depth that boosted the replay and competitive values of the whole genre to new heights.

Street Fighter II was a huge and long-lasting success in the arcades and was then ported to many home-based systems. The SNES conversion, for example, was particularly well received by the specialized press, which hailed it with enthusiastic statements like "comparing any other fighting game to *Street Fighter II* would be like comparing a game of Tic-Tac-Toe to Chess."[20]

Neverwinter Nights (1991, Stormfront Studios / SSI)

Designed by Don Daglow and released for MS-DOS-based PCs, *Neverwinter Nights* was the first title under the *Advanced Dungeons & Dragons* (AD&D) series of RPGs to go online with a "pay to play" model. Servers were hosted by America Online (AOL), which soon used the game as a useful promotional tool due to its success.

While online RPGs already had a long history by 1991,[21] *Neverwinter Nights* was the first that actually offered a proper GUI and a graphical representation of different

---

[20] Review by Piermarco Rosa published on ConsoleMania, September 1992, page 51.

[21] Roy Trubshaw started working on *MUD (Multi-User Dungeon)* in 1978 while studying at the University of Essex. The game ran on the university local network first and then spread to ARPANet in 1980, as soon as the university joined the worldwide network.

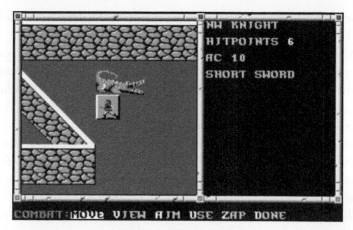

A screenshot from *Neverwinter Nights*, the first online RPG to display graphics. The game servers remained active until 1997 with each server's load increasing from as few as 50 players in 1991 up to 500 concurrent users by 1995.

environments for players to explore and coexist in. This, together with the support of players' guilds, successfully broadened the appeal of the genre and captivated many new players. Modern massively multiplayer online role-playing games (MMORPG) were born.

Doom (1993, ID Software)

December 10, 1993: the history of PC games can be divided into two eras—before and after this date, the release of *Doom*. Such was the impact of this game created by

As a space marine, the player had the duty to destroy all of the demonic creatures that were invading the moons, Phobos and Deimos. The bloody killing of monsters was never so much fun thanks to a huge variety of weapons and environments that made every new level a new discovery and challenge.

John Carmack, John Romero, and others at ID Software, that it singlehandedly managed to change the whole industry in many respects.

From a technical perspective, *Doom's* engine was a significant step up compared to earlier examples like *Wolfenstein 3D*. Environments were no longer limited to simple, regularly-shaped rooms anymore but also included stairs, lifts, and outdoor areas. Walls could now be set at any angle, allowing for interesting architectural models that made level design much more intriguing and challenging.

Doom's importance didn't stop with the game itself, however revolutionary it might have been—it was also far reaching in many other areas. Thanks to *Doom*, the shareware model affirmed itself as a viable option for developers; the first level of the game, in fact, was freely downloadable and soon became extremely popular.[22] Finally, digital distribution affirmed itself as a revolutionary way to reach customers anywhere and *Doom* successfully sold millions of units worldwide.

Additionally, LAN and modem games among four players were also possible, creating exciting head-to-head challenges between friends. Even more importantly, *Doom* also allowed for user-generated content. By distributing a level editor (aptly named DoomEd), players were allowed to become level designers and make their own maps. While *Doom* wasn't the first game to do so (*Lode Runner* by Douglas E. Smith, published by Broderbund, and *Pinball Construction Set* by Bill Budge, published by Electronic Arts, offered this in 1983), now, thanks to the Internet, people were able to easily share their own levels with friends and strangers alike, making the whole creation process much more fun and rewarding. Indeed, the roots of many game designers of today can be traced back to designing levels on DoomEd.

---

[22] *Doom* is also considered responsible for helping to spread the use of the Internet in that many computer users decided to subscribe to internet service providers (ISP) just to download and play the game.

Epilogue

Game Over

· · · · · · · ·

In the late eighties, after having brought Atari back into profitable territory again, Jack Tramiel decided to reduce his direct involvement and enjoy a well-deserved retirement. The main leading roles were then passed on to his son Sam who became both CEO and President of Atari Corp.

While the revamped 2600 Jr. and the Atari 7800 were released in 1986, the company's energies remained focused on home computers, with the ST as the most successful product.[23] Nonetheless, Atari was always caught in an uneasy situation. For most people, the name "Atari" remained synonymous with "video games" and, while losing ground to Nintendo and Sega in the entertainment sector, the company wasn't really able to change its image completely into a "respectable" computer manufacturer where the Commodore Amiga was still outselling the ST worldwide by a 3:2 ratio.

Despite these worries, 1987 was actually a very good year for the new Atari, which earned $57 million on sales that neared $500 million but, by the end of 1988, it was clear that a new, more aggressive involvement in video games was required in order to remain profitable. Instead of investing in R&D for a new home console, though, Atari decided to try a quicker route and, in December 1988, sued Nintendo for $250 million claiming that its overly restrictive licensing policies monopolized the market. Nintendo responded to Atari's suit with a countersuit charging copyright infringement and, in the end, Nintendo won in court with huge legal losses for Atari.

By the end of 1989, earnings shrunk to only $4.02 million and the situation started to get critical with not only the Amiga but also the IBM PC ramping up the competition on the home computer scene. At the same time, the new color handheld gaming console, Lynx, failed to compete successfully with the much cheaper Game Boy by Nintendo, partially due to a shortage of parts that forced it to miss the 1989 holiday season.

Atari was in serious trouble. To remain competitive, new computer models, including notebooks, were released, while a powerful pair of new products, the Falcon 030 computer system and a video gaming console, were in the works. The first version of

---

[23] Overall, the Atari ST line of computers sold approximately four million units worldwide.

The Atari Jaguar, the last gaming console from Atari Corp. Less than 250,000 units were sold.

the latter was a 32-bit machine codenamed Panther, but the project was soon abandoned in favor of a more powerful system nicknamed Jaguar. Despite all the efforts and cost-cutting measures, though, 1992 closed with a loss of $73 million and it soon became clear that the fate of the company was actually lying in the Jaguar's paws.

Manufactured by IBM for $500 million, the first sets of Jaguar hit the shelves in November 1993 and, touting an impressive 64-bit architecture, it was ready to successfully take over the older SNES and Sega Genesis. Unfortunately, the Jaguar was not a very developer-friendly machine to program and had a relatively high price tag of $250, alienating both developers and consumers alike. This, together with the industry's changing landscape due to the imminent release of the Sony PlayStation in 1994, left the Jaguar hopelessly behind in the race for success. Indeed, Sam Tramiel was well aware that the PlayStation could have killed his new machine and even vowed to go to court if Sony launched it for under $300. It actually launched at $299 and no litigation followed, but the stress may have been too high for Sam who soon suffered a heart attack.

With his son forced to step down for health reasons, Jack had to come back and seal the fate of the company. In early 1996, Atari Corp. was merged with JTS Corporation, a San Jose-based disk drive maker. Atari's staff was reduced by 80% and its assets were liquidated. Some Atari titles lived on thanks to licensing agreements with Sega but, by the end of the year, Atari's quarter-century history as a video entertainment pioneer had sadly come to an end.[24]

Commodore, on the other hand, didn't suffer Atari's image problems of being perceived as an "old video game manufacturer" but had to face other critical issues. Despite the Amiga's success, Jack Tramiel's departure left Commodore without clear leadership that Irving Gould wasn't able to fill.

---

[24] Unfortunately, JTS was short-lived and the Atari brand plus its historical IP rights were bought by Hasbro Interactive in 1998 for only $5 million. Hasbro Interactive, including all Atari rights, was then purchased by Infogrames in early 2001.

In 1992, in an effort to save on production costs on the company's entry level machine, the best-selling Amiga 500 was replaced with an inferior model, the Amiga 600, which lacked important features that severely limited its expandability. Even though the high-end Amiga models remained greatly appreciated, the lack of a clear direction for Amiga's future encouraged many developers to shift towards the IBM PC and Apple Macintosh computers whose market shares were now rapidly expanding across a more widespread crowd thanks to their improved multimedia capabilities.

A very challenging time for the former home computer leader was clearly ahead. Like Atari, Commodore desperately needed a new hit and, since the computer market was dangerously shifting away, they tried to get more into the gaming arena by converting the Amiga into a dedicated system, the Amiga CD32. The CD32 was released in September 1993 and was the first 32-bit CD-ROM-based gaming console to be released in Europe, Australia, and Canada. Notwithstanding this achievement, it wasn't able to compete with the much more popular and established SNES and Genesis and it wasn't able to face the upcoming competition from the next generation of consoles that was just around the corner. The CD32 was a commercial failure and the once mighty Commodore had to declare bankruptcy on April 29, 1994, liquidating all of its assets.

The Amiga CD32 featured a Motorola 68020 clocked at 14.3 MHz, like the Amiga 1200, but sold only about 100,000 units.

Despite the sad demise of both Atari and Commodore, their flagship systems, like the VCS, ST, C64, and Amiga series, retained a cult following for many years. Even today, they have an active "homebrew" and demo scene that is still developing amazing games, audio-visual presentations, and other software able to push the different platforms towards their limits and beyond.

Press Start to Continue

• • • • • • • • • • • • • • •

Even with Commodore and Atari gone, the gaming scene was quite healthy. PC gaming was on the rise and a new generation of dedicated consoles rocked the world once again.

Sony, after the failed collaboration with Nintendo, decided not only to enter the gaming market on its own but also to conquer it in the shortest time possible. The PlayStation console was ready to hit the shelves for the 1994 holiday season and it met with immediate success among the public, media, and developers alike.

The reasons for PlayStation's long-lasting and terrific success were several, starting from a very carefully planned strategy that included the formation of a new company branch. Sony Computer Entertainment, Inc. (SCEI)[25] officially started its operations in November 1993 to attract specific talent and to provide a more focused environment in which to work. Indeed, Sony's aim was extremely clear—to design and develop the most powerful gaming console ever, with a strong focus on 3D graphics. Raw hardware power alone wasn't enough, though, and to overpower the competition, Sony also had to have the best games not just the best hardware.

To lure the most talented developers, several tech demos were programmed by internal teams and shown to software houses worldwide. This direct and friendly approach, together with the decision to adopt CD-ROM instead of cartridges as

The original Sony PlayStation, the first home console powerful enough to handle 3D graphics easily thanks to a R3000 RISC CPU and a customized GPU.

---

[25] The previous gaming R&D work was actually carried under the Sony Music name.

the game medium to make manufacturing easier and cheaper, succeeded in raising an unprecedented interest—250 third-party developers were signed in Japan alone and all big companies like Electronic Arts, Namco, Konami, and Williams decided to support the newborn system. Sony was also active in buying specific studios to turn them into first-party developers. For example, after its impressive string of successes including *Shadow of the Beast* and *Lemmings*, UK-based Psygnosis was bought for $48 million and went on to produce some of PlayStation's best games, including titles like *WipeOut* and *Destruction Derby*.

With such enthusiasm from developers, it wasn't difficult for Sony's marketing team to transmit such positive vibes to consumers. By distancing itself from the previously dominant "family friendly" marketing approach that characterized companies such as Atari and Nintendo, Sony decided to aggressively target tech-thirsty teenagers instead. The focus shifted to the system's prowess to showcase games with more mature content, effectively enlarging the gaming audience to a new category of people who might not have been home-gamers before.

On December 3, 1994, when the first batch of consoles went on sale in Japan, long lines formed in front of every shop despite the steep price of 37,000 ¥ (about $387), turning the PlayStation into the most important product released by Sony since the WalkMan in the late 1970s. The success was indeed embraced worldwide and the PlayStation was destined to be the first system to sell more than 100 million units, making Sony the leading player in the gaming industry for years to come.

Interestingly, Sony's sudden rise to success appeared to have taken the other established console manufacturers by surprise, as evidenced by their inability to properly plan for a new strategy to effectively counter Sony's disruptive move. Sega in particular, after the impressive results obtained with the Mega Drive/Genesis, fell short in preparing for their new system, in part due to a severe lack of communication between the Japanese and American branches of the company. In fact, the former was so secretive about their new Saturn console that the latter, unaware that the Japanese headquarters was actually already designing a new system, started a parallel project on their

"It's more powerful than God," claimed one of the ads supporting Sony's marketing campaign. Together with the mascot "polygon man," it showed Sony's willingness to address the teenage crowd in a much more direct and aggressive style than ever before.

own to extend the lifespan of the Genesis. In late 1994, Sega of America released a new Genesis add-on, the 32X, which featured two 32-bit RISC processors able to increase performance and allow the development of more complex games. With the Japanese release of the Saturn scheduled around the same time, though, the lifespan of the new add-on was very short; no one, in fact, was really interested in another add-on when the next-gen system had a worldwide release just a few months later, in mid-1995.

Unfortunately, the Saturn also fell short of expectations as developers were confused by its dual CPU architecture and flocked toward Sony. In another dubious move, Sega soon admitted defeat in the current generation of consoles and decided to focus on a new system instead, leaving the Saturn to its own unlucky destiny.[26] But before having a look at what Sega had in mind, we should first see how Nintendo decided to fight back against the new threat.

Most likely, Nintendo, having been the market leader for the past two generations of consoles, felt quite secure in its dominant position and didn't really feel the need for changing much in its approach. In 1996, its new system was finally available—the Nintendo 64 (N64).

The N64 was the last contender of its generation and, while being the most technologically advanced in several respects, it also showed some serious hardware flaws and old-fashioned design choices that hampered its chances of competing against the revolutionary, and now dominant, PlayStation. First and foremost, the system was still cartridge-based. Nintendo, unlike its competitors, refused to adopt the new CD-ROM medium. While this allowed much stricter and effective control over its software and also helped in limiting possible piracy, it offered only 64 MB available to developers and at a much higher production cost. CD-ROMs were much cheaper and offered over 600 MB to include more assets, full motion videos, music, etc.,

The Nintendo 64, the last home cartridge-based system, launched in 1996 for $199 along with two titles: *Super Mario 64* and *Pilotwings 64*.

---

[26] The Sega Saturn sold less than 10 million units worldwide—only one third of the Genesis.

giving the impression to the casual player that N64 games were necessarily inferior due to size limitations.

Unfortunately, this impression was indirectly confirmed by another unlucky design choice. To keep costs down, Nintendo opted for a 4 MB unified memory architecture, meaning that the N64 had no fast, dedicated video RAM. To make things even worse, the cache memory available for textures was limited to only 4 KB. All of this resulted in generally slow performance due to the RAM high access latency and forced programmers to stretch small textures to cover large areas, often resulting in simple and blurred backgrounds. Despite these issues, developers' ingenuity still allowed for the making of fantastic games. *Super Mario 64* sold more than 11 million units and even excellent first-person shooter (FPS) titles like *GoldenEye 007* were released with critical acclaim.

Released in 1997, *GoldenEye 007* by Rare (at that time known as Rareware) was considered by many to be the best FPS game of its generation.

However, many developers still preferred to join forces with Sony, with the final result that only 387 games were released for the N64 while around 1,100 games were published for the rival PlayStation. With fewer games in its catalogue, Nintendo saw its user base shrink to 32.93 million as the N64 sold only 5.54 million units in Japan, 20.63 million in the Americas, and 6.75 million in other regions.

Towards the end of 1998, Sega was finally ready to challenge the competition properly and, after the previous missteps, this new system had to be successful or the historically strong Sega would be in real trouble. Interestingly, to get the best possible product, the company decided to pit two internal teams against each other and develop a prototype in parallel and independently. The new console, to be named Dreamcast, would be developed out of the better of the two prototypes. Both teams used a Hitachi SH-4 RISC CPU clocked at 200 MHz, but one team opted for a Videologic PowerVR2 graphics processor while the other chose hardware by 3dfx, which was the leading PC graphic card manufacturer at the time. At first, the latter encountered more favorable feedback but, due to an in-principle agreement between Sega and 3dfx that was completely disclosed during 3dfx's own initial public offering, it was ultimately decided to opt for the former. As a consequence, 3dfx's value as a company was shattered[27] and the Dreamcast was left with what was probably an inferior design.

The Dreamcast launched in November 1998 in Japan without much excitement, but the North American debut on September 9, 1999, was a great success. Thanks also to a solid line-up of titles, including the likes of *Soul Calibur* and *Sonic Adventure* among others, the Dreamcast had a very good start. Sega sold 500,000 consoles in just two weeks, including a record 225,132 during the first 24 hours, and after its first price cut in mid-2000, it actually passed the N64 in terms of sales for a few months.

The Dreamcast was truly a pioneering product thanks to its internal modem and online playing capabilities, but the times were not mature enough yet for such technologies. Internet infrastructure and penetration were still gaining momentum and things started turning ugly pretty quickly. Some high profile titles like *Shenmue* (which included the planning for two sequels and an overall budget as high as $70 million) didn't perform as well as expected despite critical acclaim, and when Sony released the PlayStation 2 in 2000, it was clear who would rule the new generation of consoles.

Ultimately, Sega decided to discontinue the Dreamcast in 2001 after 10.6 million units were sold and to completely withdraw from the console hardware business to focus exclusively on software instead.

The Dreamcast, SEGA's last console and the first to include a built-in dial-up modem and Internet support for online play.

---

[27] The company was bought by Nvidia a few years later.

Thanks also to its built-in DVD player, the PlayStation 2 quickly became the most successful gaming system ever.

The PlayStation 2 (PS2) became the best selling console ever with more than 145 million units sold[28] and it greatly contributed to the development of video games into a more mature form of entertainment. Gifted game designers finally had enough power to create highly immersive and emotionally engaging titles. For example, *ICO* and *Shadow of the Colossus* by Fumito Ueda, *Okami* by Hideki Kamiya, and many others across a variety of genres like RPG, FPS, and simulations pushed games from a mere pastime to a true art form.

ICO, developed in 2001 exclusively for the PS2 by Fumito Ueda, successfully relied on the emotional connection between the player and an NPC to craft an unforgettable experience, showing that games were able to deliver more than just blasting aliens and zombies.

---

[28] As of June 20, 2010.

The Nintendo GameCube. No more cartridges this time, but a mini-DVD featuring a proprietary format with a capacity of 1.5 GB. Nintendo's total sales slipped further to 21.6 million units with this next generation offering as more gamers moved towards competing systems.

In late 2001, after Sega's demise as a hardware manufacturer, Nintendo released its next console, the GameCube, but, more importantly, the vacant space left by Sega was immediately taken by another, powerful contender: Microsoft.

The Xbox was released in North America on November 15, 2001, and worldwide by early 2002. While not able to challenge the PS2 in terms of sales, the Xbox successfully catered to the teenage crowd thanks to excellent FPS games like *Halo,* and Xbox ultimately surpassed the GameCube by selling about 24 million units.

The Xbox (2001). Online play finally became mainstream.

Interestingly, one of the main characteristics that made Microsoft's first venture into the hardware video game sector a success was the same one that wasn't able to save the Dreamcast: online play. In just a few years, Internet penetration and usage increased tremendously and, while the Dreamcast had only a slow dial-up modem, the Xbox was broadband-ready. The Xbox Live service was launched in 2002 and showed that many players really loved to challenge and to cooperate with each other online, pushing Sony and Nintendo to take steps in that direction.

This generation of consoles, besides the even higher quality and scope of games, also fostered new growth across the whole industry. Producing games became an even more serious affair—teams expanded and budgets grew accordingly, with the average title employing at least 20 people with budgets of a few million dollars while top titles could reach up to $20 million.

This trend has continued through the most recent generation of game development. The Xbox 360 was released in late 2005, with Sony's PlayStation 3 (PS3) and Nintendo's Wii following one year later. The average title by a leading publisher is now expected to involve up to 100 professionals with a budget of about $20 million, with some games reaching as high as $100 million. Having so many resources all focused on a single project has turned the industry into a "hit driven" affair where a single miss can seriously endanger a company's future and the jobs of hundreds of professionals. This, in turn, has had the consequence of fostering the creativity of small groups of independent developers who made originality their main weapon, and creative freedom their ultimate goal. The "indie" scene, as these groups are generally referred to, aims to create unconventional titles while experimenting with new business models on a variety of platforms. Free of the constraints that have to be enforced in big corporations, these groups have met with considerable success and recognition during the last few years.

Grand Theft Auto IV, published by Take Two Interactive and developed by Rock Star Games for the Xbox 360, PS3, and PC platform, employed about 150 people and had a total budget of around $100 million, making it the most expensive title ever made up to this point. The game sold more than 17 million copies overall.

The Nintendo Wii and its motion-based Wiimote controller. By selling more than 70 million units, it brought a fresh, new perspective of gaming to hundreds of millions of people worldwide and helped Nintendo regain its leadership position in the industry. [29]

Overall, during the last generation where online play is considered a sine qua non for successful gaming, innovation moved towards providing a different experience thanks to motion controllers. These were successfully introduced in the mass market by the Nintendo Wii and then enhanced further by Sony and Microsoft with their Move and Kinect add-ons released in late 2010 for their respective consoles.

What will the future bring us? Only time will tell.

---

[29] As of June 30, 2010, Wii sales were 73.97 million units, followed by the Xbox 360 with 41.7 million and the PS3 with 38.1 million.

Appendix A

• • • • • • • •

A Brief History of Handheld Devices

Interestingly, the history of handheld electronic gaming devices is almost as long as that of their arcade and home counterparts. After a first experiment by Waco in 1972 with a tic-tac-toe game, it was Mattel in 1977 that seriously pushed into the market by releasing its first dedicated handheld game, *Auto Race*. This, followed by *Football* and other sports-based titles, was met with great success by the general public and proved that electronic and video games could be a viable product "on the go" and not only in homes or at the arcades.

Coleco, Milton Bradley, and others soon followed Mattel and the handheld market started becoming a lively and growing segment in the gaming industry alongside the home sector. Milton Bradley, in particular, was responsible for the first cartridge-based handheld: the Microvision, released in 1979. Unfortunately, the Microvision was an extremely fragile device and both the system and games were prone to break very easily, seriously stifling its chances of success.

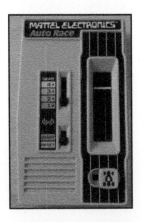

Mattel's *Auto Race* was the first fully electronic handheld game ever released and ran through a very simple LED display system and 512 bytes of memory.

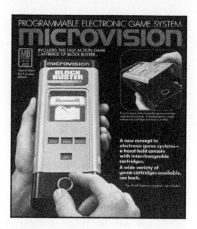

The Microvision—the first cartridge-based system having a display of only 16 × 16 pixels. It was released in October 1979, and then discontinued in less than two years due to its poor success.

To find the next successful series of products, let's shift to Japan where, from 1980 onwards, Nintendo decided to follow up its early successes with a set of simple electronic games based on LCD screens—the *Game & Watch* series was born. Designed by Gunpei Yokoi, *Game & Watch* was a clear breakthrough for Nintendo and helped to define many elements that became commonplace in later systems, both handheld and home based, like the D-Pad. Different series were produced till 1991 and are now coveted collector's items.

Also in Japan, in 1984 Epoch tried to develop another cartridge-based handheld, named Game Pocket Computer. This time, the screen had a resolution of 76 × 64 pixels but the technology of the time was not yet mature enough to deliver complex experiences on the go.

Donkey Kong in its *Game & Watch* incarnation dating back to 1982. Note the D-Pad and the dual screen, which were later adopted in the NES and the Nintendo DS, respectively.

The Game Boy retailed for $89.99 and was an instant success. The display size was 160 × 144 pixels and it featured an 8-bit LR35902 CPU by Sharp that merged the best of the Intel 8080 and Zilog Z-80 processors, delivering enough power for the development of fun and addictive games.

It was only in 1989, and again thanks to Nintendo and Gunpei Yokoi, that handheld gaming was finally able to move to its next generation as a result of the popularity of the Game Boy. The Game Boy was an instant success, thanks also to its being bundled with *Tetris*. Across its multiple iterations and restylings like the Game Boy Pocket and Game Boy Color, it sold more than 118 million units worldwide.

Such instant and staggering success excited many other companies and the handheld market started getting crowded very fast. The first challenger was Atari, which, in 1989, released the Lynx by implementing a previous prototype developed by Epyx in 1987.

Designed by Alexey Pajitnov, *Tetris* found a perfect platform in the Game Boy. Thanks to this very simple yet addictive action/puzzle game, the Game Boy was successful in attracting not only youngsters but also a more adult crowd.

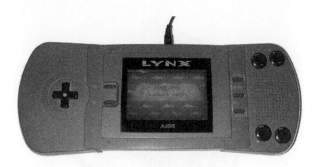

The Atari Lynx was the first handheld with a backlit and color screen. Built around a MOS 6502 CPU, it was released in 1989 at $189.99 and needed six AA batteries for just a few hours of playing time. Overall, it sold less than five million units.

Despite its technical qualities, the Lynx had all the same issues that would soon plague other upcoming devices like the NEC Turbo Express (1990, a portable TurboGrafx-16), the Sega Game Gear (1990),[30] Nomad (1995), and others, preventing them from being able to compete seriously against Nintendo. In particular, poor battery life, big clunky size, and a much higher price tag all contributed to diminishing their appeal to a crowd for which all of these characteristics were more important than raw power for a device to be used while not at home. At the same time, Nintendo, thanks to its dominant position in the market and the doubtful strategies implemented by its competitors, was able to maintain its leadership comfortably by gradually releasing new iterations of its device that featured small, but meaningful, technical improvements[31] together with more ergonomic designs.

The strategy of pleasing its audience thanks to small incremental improvements while delaying a more robust next generation until the underlying technology would be more affordable—and thereby maintaining high profit margins—proved successful and the Game Boy Advance was not released until 2001.[32] Following this, though, Nintendo, decided to release its next console, the Nintendo DS, in 2004, probably in anticipation of the release of Sony's PlayStation Portable (PSP) in 2005. The DS was a staggering success, especially after the release of the "Lite" version in 2006, selling more than 135 million units worldwide. However, Sony was still able to seize a respectable share of the market with its PSP by selling more than 60 million units.[33]

---

[30] The Game Gear was actually the most successful among the Game Boy competitors and sold around 11 million units worldwide.

[31] The Game Boy Color, the first Nintendo handheld with a color display, wasn't released until 1998.

[32] The Game Boy Advance sold more than 81 million units overall.

[33] As of September 2010.

The original Nintendo DS as released in 2004. As with its predecessors, several iterations offering small but meaningful improvements followed within a few years, turning this device into the most successful handheld gaming system ever released.

Though an analysis of past results shows that, at any given time, only very few players are able to take a meaningful role in this industry, many small and big companies alike keep trying to carve a niche audience for themselves by providing new ideas and systems. For example, despite the marketplace becoming even riskier and more competitive after the sudden and powerful rise of Apple's iPhone/iPad platforms, companies such as South Korean Game Park Holdings succeeded in building a small but significant following by producing devices open to hobbyists to freely develop games. And tech giants like Panasonic recently announced the upcoming release of a new handheld focused on online gaming (the Jungle, planned for 2011).

At the same time, Nintendo is ready to release its new device, the 3DS, which will be able to deliver actual 3D images on the go without the need for special glasses, thereby pushing the industry and its competitiveness to new heights once again.

Appendix B

Collecting Classic Games Today

An interesting phenomenon that has grown in popularity during the last few years is the collecting of old and classic games. Many people all around the world, whether adults looking to remember their younger days or new gamers eager to know more about the history of their favorite hobby, are seeking to experience old games once again and enjoy their legacy.

Online forums and websites are very active, and meetings and conferences on the subject are regularly organized around the world. Through a variety of means, the dedication of so many enthusiasts has successfully turned forgotten pieces of plastic and electronics into valuable collectibles that can fetch very high prices on popular auction sites.

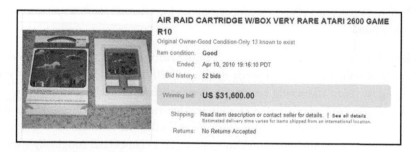

On April 10, 2010, an extremely rare game for the Atari 2600, *Air Raid*, sold for $31,600 on the popular auction site eBay.

An Interview with Mike Kennedy

To understand more about classic games collecting, we interviewed Mike Kennedy. Mike is the founder and CEO of GameGavel.com, the cohost of the RetroGamingRoundup, a monthly podcast on retro games, and, obviously, an avid game collector and expert on this subject.

Roberto Dillon: *Hello Mike, can you tell us something about yourself and how games came to play a significant role in your life?*

Mike Kennedy: I grew up in the 70s and 80s. So, obviously, video and arcade gaming played a big part in my childhood. Unlike for many of my friends, gaming has continued to play a big role in my life—so much so that I have started a business centered on this lifestyle (yes, lifestyle) that I love so much. I started gaming, like many of us, in the arcades and on the Atari 2600 at home. Soon I moved onto computers, owning first a Timex Sinclair 1000 and moving quickly onto the Commodore 64 and ultimately to an Apple IIc when I was in high school. So, I had a good mix of arcade, console, and computer gaming while growing up. Fast forward to today. With the advent of the Internet as well as the weekly swap meets year round here in Southern California, I have been able to go back and experience all the games and gaming systems I didn't have as a child. I currently own pretty much all the classic gaming systems from the Atari 2600, Intellivision, ColecoVision, Odyssey 2, NES, SNES, Sega Master System, Genesis and Dreamcast, Vectrex, and TurboGrafx right through the current generation systems, the Nintendo Wii and the PS3. I love mobile gaming as well on my Nintendo DS, GBA, GP2X, iPod/iPad, etc. In addition to console gaming, I also spend lots of time in our home arcade playing some of the arcade and pinball games that I dropped so many quarters into back in the day.

RD: *How and why did you get the idea of starting GameGavel? How many users does it currently have?*

Mike: I had been a pretty regular eBay member since 1997 so I had a good understanding of online auctions. Towards the end of 2007, I could tell that eBay was changing its vision and would be making changes that were really going to turn me off. I was trying to find other places to buy and sell video games and realized that the options were pretty limited. So, I decided to deal eBay the ultimate blow and start an auction site dedicated only to video gaming, and GameGavel (originally named ChaseTheChuckwagon.com) was born on March 24, 2008. To give back to the community and to the hobby that I love, I wanted to make an auction site that was similar enough to eBay in its appearance but featured a less expensive environment to sell on. So, I made the decision to do away with listing fees and then cut the eBay selling/final value fees and commissions in half. The bottom line is that, for sellers, it is a much cheaper place to sell their items. Since launching the auction site, I have added other community features such as gaming forums, industry blogs, a retrogaming-themed streaming radio station (http://www.retroarcaderadio.com) and we have also spun off a monthly retrogaming podcast (http://www.retrogamingroundup.com). Overall, GameGavel is more than a video game auction site, but rather a unique, all-inclusive gaming destination where gamers can buy and sell, and also mingle and catch up on the latest industry news and opinions. There is really nothing else like it anywhere. Currently, after about two and a half years, GameGavel has nearly 5,000 members and is visited monthly by over 50,000 unique visitors. It has hosted over 300,000 gaming auctions and sold nearly $200,000 in merchandise.

RD: *Is vintage game collecting a hobby that has spread mostly in North America or do you think it is also getting more popular worldwide?*

Mike: Again, with the dawn of the Internet, I think vintage gaming is a worldwide interest. I think it appears to be predominantly a North American hobby, maybe because a lot of the earliest forms of gaming were invented here in the United States, at least until after the crash of 1983 when Japanese companies Nintendo and Sega established themselves as the new leaders of the industry. But for the most part, gamers want to experience lots of things they missed out on during the first go-around. And now it is easier than ever to collect a variety of vintage gaming systems from all around the world.

RD: *What do you think makes it so attractive? Why do so many people see game carts from previous console generations as not just old pieces of plastic?*

Mike: A lot of the gamers who grew up in the advent of gaming are obviously much older now and have some discretionary income. What better things to buy than video games? It is a relatively inexpensive hobby that has the ability to transport people back to their younger days with the flip of a switch and the twitch of a joystick. There is no shortage of gaming systems and memorabilia to collect. And you can take your collecting as far as you want to. Do you want to go after the expensive rare games or prototypes? Or just try to complete a collection of the more common less expensive games? It is your choice and there is a level for about any collector's budget out there. There is just so much you can collect, from the systems themselves to the games, and the loads of gaming toys and memorabilia that has come out over the years.

RD: *What suggestions would you give to someone who wants to start a new collection?*

Mike: First, you have to decide how much money you want to spend and if you are going to be a hardcore collector who has to have every game made for a system, or a more passive collector who is happy just picking and choosing games to their liking. If you fall into the hardcore, gotta-have-it-all category, to begin I would recommend starting a collection with a system that is easy to collect—perhaps a system like the Atari 5200 or the Odyssey 2. Both systems have a smaller game catalog as compared to some of the other systems like the Atari 2600 or Nintendo NES. If you are passive, like me, then you simply pick up the games you remember or had as a child. Or games that you would have liked to have owned back in the day, but missed out on. Personally, I like to spread my collecting around a variety of systems, not just a single system.

RD: *Which games and platforms are particularly sought after nowadays?*

Mike: Right now, it really depends on the various generations of gamers. I believe that the dawn of collecting the first generation systems has reached its peak and is on the decline. Most collectors of this earliest era have been collecting for the past 10 years or so and have what they want, or are chasing rare or more out-of-reach games. Today, I think the second generation of gamers is leading the way, collecting for the Nintendo and Sega systems from the mid to late 80s to mid-90s. It is cyclical and soon the third generation collectors will be trying to find the sought-after Sony PlayStation, Nintendo 64, and Sega Dreamcast games they grew up with.

RD: *There have been items that fetched very high prices in online auctions. Do you think this trend will continue or have these been one-hit wonders that will likely not be repeated in the future?*

Mike: I think that is anyone's guess. But I believe now is a peak time for collectors of the earliest first generation systems. It is a key time where most of us are in our early 40s and our collecting goals and income is at an all-time high. So I think for now, rare games and systems from the first generation will continue to hit their highest prices, but as each year goes by I think prices will decline. Now the second generation of system collectors is maturing and rarities for the Nintendo NES through the SNES, Genesis, and N64 will rise in value, and then fall. And so on. It is important for gamers to continue collecting as they age, and to introduce these classic systems to their children and to their children's friends. Keep classic gaming alive from the first generation of systems right through to the present day, some way, somehow. If someone is getting out of collecting, sell or give your collection to someone else. Don't throw it away. We must preserve all that we can.

Bibliography

• • • • • • • • •

Ralph Baer. *Videogames: In The Beginning*. Springfield, NJ: Rolenta Press, 2005.

Brian Bagnall. *Commodore: A Company on the Edge*. Second ed. Winnipeg, Manitoba: Variant Press, 2010.

Ian Bogost and Nick Montfort. *Racing the Beam: The Atari Video Computer System*. Cambridge, MA: MIT Press, 2009.

Van Burnham. *Supercade: A Visual History of the Videogame Age 1971–1984*. Cambridge, MA: MIT Press, 2003.

Scott Cohen. *Zap!: The Rise and Fall of Atari*. New York, NY: McGraw-Hill, 1984.

Tristan Donovan. *Replay: The History of Video Games*. Sussex, UK: Yellow Ant Media, 2010.

Rusel DeMaria and Johnny Wilson. *High Score!: The Illustrated History of Electronic Games*. Second Ed. New York, NY: McGraw-Hill Osborne Media, 2004.

Jerry Ellis. *The 8-Bit Book: 1981-199x*. Loachapoka, AL: Hiive Books, 2010.

Andrew Fisher. *The Commodore 64 Book: 1982-199x*. Loachapoka, AL: Hiive Books, 2008.

Leonard Herman. *Phoenix: The Fall and Rise of Videogames*. Springfield, NJ: Rolenta Press, 1994.

Steven L. Kent. *The Ultimate History of Video Games*. New York, NY: Three Rivers Press, 2001.

Chris Kohler. *Power-Up: How Japanese Video Games Gave the World an Extra Life*. Indianapolis, IN: BradyGames, 2004.

Andrew Rollings. *The ZX Spectrum Book: 1982-199x*, Loachapoka, AL: Hiive Books, 2007.

Michael Tomczyk. *The Home Computer Wars: An Insider's Account of Commodore and Jack Tramiel*. Greensboro, NC: Compute! Publications, 1984.

Brett Weiss. *Classic Home Video Games, 1972-1984: A Complete Reference Guide*. Jefferson, NC: McFarland & Company, 2007.

—. *Classic Home Video Games 1985-1988: A Complete Reference Guide*. Second ed. Jefferson, NC: McFarland & Company, 2009.

Robert Wicker and Jason Brassard. *Classic 80s Home Video Games*. Third ed. Padukah, KY: Collector Books, 2008.

Online resources (accessed on September 1, 2010):
    www.klov.com
    www.arcadeflyers.com
    www.pong-story.com
     www.old-computers.com
    www.oldcomputers.net
    www.atarihq.com
    www.wikipedia.org
    www.retro-gaming.it
    www.retromags.com
    www.apple2history.org
    www.vgchartz.com
    www.gameconsoles.com
    www.mobygames.com
    www.thedoteaters.com
    www.vintagecomputing.com

Photo Credits

• • • • • • • • • •

Index

• • • •

About the Author

• • • • • • • • • • • •

Roberto Dillon was born in Genoa, Italy, in 1973. In 1981, he had his first encounter with a home computer, a Texas Instruments 99/4A, and then with an Intellivision gaming console. In 1983, he received a Commodore 64 that hooked him into technology, computer science, and games ever since.

He holds a Master and a Ph.D. degree in Electrical and Computer Engineering from the University of Genoa and, after having worked both in the software/multimedia development industry and in prestigious academic institutions across Europe and Asia, he joined the Singapore campus of the DigiPen Institute of Technology where he is currently an Assistant Professor lecturing on a variety of game design subjects including Game Mechanics and Game History.

Roberto has led high profile research projects on innovative game mechanics and designed serious, educational, and experimental games that were showcased internationally in newspapers like *USA Today* and at events like the Sense of Wonder Night within the Tokyo Game Show.

He is the author of *On the Way to Fun: An Emotion-Based Approach to Successful Game Design*, published by A K Peters, Ltd. in 2010 and he can be contacted through his website *www.ProgramAndPlay.com*.